I0413284

Detection of Environmental DNA of Bigheaded Carps in Samples Collected from Selected Locations in the St. Croix River and in the Mississippi River

By Jon J. Amberg, Sunnie G. McCalla, Loren Miller, Peter Sorensen and Mark P. Gaikowski

Prepared in collaboration with the University of Minnesota

Open-File Report 2013–1080

U.S. Department of the Interior
U.S. Geological Survey

U.S. Department of the Interior
KEN SALAZAR, Secretary

U.S. Geological Survey
Suzette M. Kimball, Acting Director

U.S. Geological Survey, Reston, Virginia: 2013

For more information on the USGS—the Federal source for science about the Earth, its natural and living resources, natural hazards, and the environment, visit http://www.usgs.gov or call 1–888–ASK–USGS.

For an overview of USGS information products, including maps, imagery, and publications, visit http://www.usgs.gov/pubprod

To order this and other USGS information products, visit http://store.usgs.gov

Financial Disclosure
The analyses described in this interim report were fully funded by the Environment and Natural Resources Trust Fund through a grant to the University of Minnesota and through a Collaborative Agreement between the University of Minnesota and the U.S. Geological Survey.

Contents

Figures

Detection of Environmental DNA of Bigheaded Carps in Samples Collected from Selected Locations in the St. Croix River and in the Mississippi River

By Jon J. Amberg[1], Sunnie G. McCalla[1], Loren Miller[2,3], Peter Sorensen[3] and Mark P. Gaikowski[1]

Background

The use of molecular methods, such as the detection of environmental deoxyribonucleic acid (eDNA), have become an increasingly popular tool in surveillance programs that monitor for the presence of invasive species in aquatic systems. One early application of these methods in aquatic systems was surveillance for DNA of Asian carps (specifically bighead carp *Hypophthalmichthys nobilis* and silver carp *H. molitrix*) in water samples taken from the Chicago Area Waterway System (CAWS; Jerde et al. 2011). Analysis of water samples from the CAWS to detect DNA of Asian carps has since been integrated into the Asian carp monitoring program managed by the Monitoring and Response Work Group, an interagency group established by the Asian Carp Regional Coordinating Committee. The U.S. Army Corps of Engineers (USACE) is presently responsible for the analysis of DNA in samples taken from the CAWS and has led the development and refinement of the methods and procedures used to process environmental samples to detect Asian carp DNA. Those methods are specified within the USACE "Quality Assurance Project Plan" or QAPP (USACE 2012).

The ability to identify DNA of a species in an environmental sample presents a potentially powerful tool to detect the leading edges of the invasion front of invasive animals such as Asian carp. Surveillance programs that incorporate eDNA monitoring have the potential for greater detection power because these sensitive analyses can presumably detect the presence of DNA in water even when the species is not abundant (Jerde et al. 2011). An initial eDNA surveillance effort was completed in Minnesota waters in 2011 after the capture of a bighead carp in the St. Croix River near Prescott, WI. Samples collected and analyzed for the presence of Asian carp DNA were expected to delineate the invasion front of bighead and silver carp in the Mississippi River and St. Croix River (Hickox et al. 2011; Hsu et al. 2011). The presence of silver carp DNA in samples collected in 2011 triggered a response by the Minnesota Department of Natural Resources (MN DNR) to intensively sample with conventional fishing gear areas where silver carp DNA was detected and to complete additional eDNA sampling and analysis. Although presumptive silver carp DNA was measured in several samples in the St. Croix and Mississippi Rivers, only two silver carp have since been captured in the Mississippi, and then downstream of the sampling locations, in the past two years (USGS 2013). Several bighead carp have also been captured by fishermen.

The environmental samples taken in 2011 for DNA analysis were processed by a private contractor using the markers identified in Jerde et al. (2011); PCR-positive samples were confirmed to contain the DNA of bighead carp or silver carp using a hybridization technique rather than sequencing as prescribed by the USACE QAPP. Subsequent to the 2011 eDNA sampling and analysis efforts, multiple pathways (e.g. fish-eating birds, commercial fishing gear) have been identified that could transfer DNA within aquatic systems (USACE 2013). The potential transfer of Asian carp DNA through vectors or fomites from locations where Asian carp are abundant to locations where they are absent or at low density might produce variable levels of basal DNA that would complicate interpretation of any silver carp or bighead carp DNA from a live fish. This study had several goals. The University, per its contract with the Environmental and Natural Resources Trust Fund (ENRTF), was primarily interested in determining if previous results from the Mississippi and St. Croix Rivers could be duplicated and were thus credible. It was secondarily interested in gaining critical insight into the nature of the QAPP technique so that recommendations for future work could be made to the MN DNR. We specifically sought to understand the potential confounding effects of these other pathways on this variation in background DNA by collecting water samples from (1) sites within the St. Croix River and the Mississippi River where the DNA of silver carp was previously detected,

[1]United States Geological Survey, Upper Midwest Environmental Sciences Center (UMESC), 2630 Fanta Reed Road, La Crosse, WI 54603

[2]Minnesota Department of Natural Resources, Department of Fisheries, Wildlife and Conservation Biology, University of Minnesota, 1980 Folwell Avenue, St. Paul, MN 55018

[3]University of Minnesota (UMN),

(2) sites considered to be free of Asian carp, and (3) a site known to have a large population of Asian carp. We also sought to establish a baseline Asian carp eDNA signature to which future eDNA sampling efforts could be compared. All samples described in this report were processed according to procedures of the USACE QAPP with seven exceptions designed to render the final analysis more definitive.

Water samples (Table 1) were collected from (1) sites similar to those sampled during the eDNA survey completed in 2011 (MN DNR 2011), (2) two Asian carp-free lakes that were expected to serve as negative controls, and (3) from the Mississippi River below Lock and Dam 19. Samples were collected below Lock and Dam 19 to serve as a positive control and to determine the DNA detection frequency, i.e., the frequency of detecting DNA in locations with high carp abundance. The negative control sites were expected to either not contain Asian carp DNA or to provide insight on potential background noise associated with the transfer of DNA from alternate pathways.

Methods

Definition of Terms Used to Report the Detection of DNA

The following terms were used to describe the detection of Asian carp DNA in environmental samples through the use of conventional polymerase chain reaction (PCR) or Sanger sequencing.

PCR – Polymerase chain reaction

Negative control samples – samples that did not contain silver carp or bighead carp DNA (i.e. cooler blanks, well water laboratory controls and DNA-free PCR controls).

Positive control samples – samples that intentionally contained silver carp or bighead carp DNA.

Presumptive PCR-positive – bands between 150 to 300 bp for silver carp or 250 to 400 bp for bighead carp observed in any of the initial 8 PCR replicates processed from an environmental sample.

Determinative PCR-positive – bands between 150 to 300 bp for silver carp or 250 to 400 bp for bighead carp observed in any of the subsequent 8 PCR replicates prepared from an environmental sample determined to be presumptive PCR-positive.

Confirmed positive – appropriately sized bands from determinative PCR-positive environmental samples were submitted for Sanger sequencing. Resulting sequences were compared with published silver carp or bighead carp sequences by Basic Local Alignment Search Tool analysis (BLAST; Altschul et al. 1997); the sample was identified as a confirmed positive only if both the forward and reverse sequences (>150 bp in length) of the amplicon were ≥95% identical to published sequences of silver carp or bighead carp.

Table 1. Sites sampled and processed as part of the collaborative agreement between USGS-UMESC and the University of Minnesota. The coordinates given are the approximate centroid of the sampling location. Fifty water samples were taken and 3 cooler blanks were prepared at each sample location. Fifty samples of well water were taken and 25 samples of a slurry of silver carp and bighead carp mucus and feces were prepared to provide negative and positive control samples during DNA extraction and PCR analysis.

Water body	Site description	Reason for sampling	Reported in Hsu et al. (2012)	Date of sample collection	Location (UTM Easting /Northing)
Square Lake	Washington County, MN	Negative control	N	10/01/2012	515976/4999913
Lake Riley	Carver County, MN	Negative control	N	10/02/2012	459498/4964912
Mississippi River	Above Coon Rapids Dam	Surveillance	Y	09/18/2012	474161/4999883
	Below Coon Rapids Dam	Surveillance	Y	09/24/2012	475840/4998776
	Below Lock and Dam 1 (Ford Dam)	Surveillance	Y	09/25/2012	485496/4971803
	Below Lock and Dam 19 (Keokuk, IA)	Positive control	N	10/16/2012	637179/4471775
St. Croix River	Above St. Croix Falls Dam	Surveillance	Y	09/17/2012	526806/5027129
	Below St. Croix Falls Dam	Surveillance	Y	09/19/2012	527077/5031622
UMESC	Well water (N=50)	Negative control	N	12/17/2012	NA
UMESC	Silver carp slurry (N=25)	Positive control	N	12/17/2012	NA
UMESC	Bighead carp slurry (N=25)	Positive control	N	3/1/2013	NA

Sample Collection

Fifty, 2-L surface water samples (surface to approximately 5 cm below surface) were collected from each of eight sites (Table 1) by targeting specific areas (eddies, below and around structures, confluence of tributaries, etc.) as well as shore samples and transects attempting to get a dispersed coverage of the sampling sites (Figures 1-8). Samples were processed according to procedures specified in the USACE QAPP by personnel from MN DNR and UMN, except that sterile, disposable funnels (Pall MicroFunnel 300) were used instead of a reusable magnetic filter funnel that must be sterilized between samples. These funnels were identical to those used in 2011 (Hickox et al. 2011; Hsu et al 2012). Cooler blanks (n=3) were prepared at each site concurrent with the collection of the 50 environmental samples. The presence of avian predators (e.g. fish-eating birds) was noted during collection of environmental samples (Appendix 1). No attempt is made by this report to link the presence of Asian carp DNA to potential avian transport of DNA from one location to another. All other sampling procedures, including the collection and handling of appropriate controls (i.e. cooler blanks), followed the procedures specified in the USACE QAPP. Each sample was filtered through a 1.5 μm glass-fiber filter; filters were placed in labeled, 50-mL conical centrifuge tubes and immediately stored at 20°C. Filters were transported on dry ice to UMESC where they were then stored at -80°C until processed to extract DNA and complete PCR analysis.

Laboratory positive control samples consisted of 25 samples of silver carp slurry prepared from silver carp mucus and fecal material and 25 samples of bighead carp slurry prepared from bighead carp mucus and fecal material. Laboratory negative control samples consisted of 50 samples of UMESC well water. All laboratory positive and negative control samples were prepared at UMESC by UMESC personnel.

DNA Extraction

The DNA adhering to filters was extracted using the MO BIO PowerWater DNA Isolation Kit (MO BIO Laboratories, Inc., Carlsbad, CA) according to the procedures specified in the USACE QAPP with certain modifications. The DNA extracted from sample filters was stored at -20°C until PCR analysis. The modifications of the USACE QAPP procedures were made to improve rigor in our sample analyses and decrease the potential for contamination and were as follows:

- Each extraction kit (one kit contained the requisite consumables to complete 100 extractions) was subdivided on receipt at UMESC into separate sets sufficient to complete 25 extractions. This reduced the risk of contamination of the consumables and reduced the risk that contamination of consumables might impact multiple sample sets.

- Extractions were completed on sets of 20 unknown samples. All preparatory surfaces were sterilized with 10% hypochlorous acid solution (bleach) or exposure to UV light (>15 minutes) between each set of 20 unknown sample extractions.

- Extracting DNA from 3 or more filters in a single PowerWater extraction increased the rate of failure of the extraction process (USACE 2013). For samples with 2 or more filters, DNA was extracted from no more than 2 filters within an extraction vessel. This modification was recently incorporated into the procedures specified in the USACE QAPP.

- A positive silver carp control sample and a negative control sample were processed with each batch of 20 extractions. This deviated from the USACE QAPP, which requires one positive and one negative control sample for every 25 extractions.

- Samples that contained Asian carp DNA following initial PCR (presumptive PCR-positive) were subjected to a second PCR analysis (in octuplet) to confirm the presence of Asian carp DNA. Samples were only considered determinative PCR-positive if Asian carp DNA was amplified in at least one of the octuplet replicates in the second PCR analysis. This deviated from the USACE QAPP that dropped the processing of the second PCR analysis. Completing the second PCR analysis provided a more rigorous approach to eliminate non-specific amplification of DNA sequences of lengths similar to the target amplicon.

- The DNA of 50% of the presumptive PCR-positives (>1 positive replicate of the 8 PCR replicates) from below Lock and Dam 19 were re-amplified. All of the determinative PCR-positives were sequenced. This deviated from the USACE QAPP which specifies that 5% of positive samples from known Asian carp waters be sequenced.

PCR Analysis

The presence of silver carp DNA or bighead carp DNA was determined by PCR using the following species specific markers: silver carp, forward CCTGARAAAAGARKTRTTCCACTATAA, reverse GCCAAATGCAAGTAATAGTTCATTC; bighead carp, forward TAACTTAAATAAACAGATTA, reverse TAAAAGAATGCTCGGCATGT. These markers (originally reported by Jerde et al. 2011) are presently used in the Asian carp eDNA surveillance program applied in the CAWS. Each sample was processed in octuplet by PCR for each species. Each run contained a positive and a negative PCR control, as well as a laboratory positive and a negative control sample. All PCR reactions (25 µL) were prepared using the reagents specified in the USACE QAPP. The PCR conditions used for the silver carp marker was initial denaturation at 94°C for 10 minutes followed by 45 cycles of 94°C for 1 minute then 50°C for 1 minute then 72°C for 1.5 minutes; there was a final extension at 72°C for 7 minutes after the 45 cycles. The PCR conditions used for the bighead carp marker were the same except that a temperature of 52°C was used instead of 50°C. The PCR products were held at 4°C until the plate was removed from the thermocycler. All original DNA extracts were stored at -20°C. The PCR products were visualized by electrophoresis on a 2% agarose gel, stained with GelRed™ (Biotium Inc., Hayward, CA, USA). The presence of the appropriate band was visualized under ultraviolet light. Any sample in which DNA of the appropriate amplicon length (i.e. ~190 bp for silver carp and ~310 bp for bighead carp) was present in one or more of the 8 PCR replicates in the initial PCR analysis was considered presumptive PCR-positive. Occasionally, bands of a similar length to that of the targeted sequences can be detected, likely due to non-specific amplification. If a band of the appropriate length was observed in any of the 8 PCR replicates of a DNA extract, the sample was re-analyzed by PCR using the process described above except that only a positive and a negative PCR control were used. Any sample in which DNA of the appropriate amplicon length was present in one or more of the 8 PCR replicates in the second PCR analysis was considered determinative PCR-positive. All samples considered presumptive PCR-positive were re-analyzed within 6 weeks of the original PCR analysis.

DNA Verification

The DNA of all determinative PCR-positive samples from any location other than below Lock and Dam 19 was eluted from the agarose gel using a QIAquick Gel Extraction Kit (QIAGEN Inc., Valencia, CA) and cleaned using a QIAquick PCR Purification Kit (QIAGEN Inc., Valencia, CA). The DNA from 50% of the determinative PCR-positives (17 of 34) from below Lock and Dam 19 was re-analyzed and any subsequent determinative PCR-positives (16 of 17) were eluted as described above. The eluted DNA was transported to the University of Minnesota Biomedical Genomics Center (St. Paul, MN) for Sanger sequencing (forward and reverse sequencing). The resulting sequences were compared using BLAST analysis to published sequences in GenBank (*http://www.ncbi.nlm.nih.gov/genbank/*). A sample was identified as a confirmed positive only if both the forward and reverse

sequences (>150 bp in length) of the amplicon were ≥95% identical to published sequences of silver carp or bighead carp.

Results

A total of 596 DNA extractions were performed from 400 environmental samples, 25 silver carp positive control samples, 25 bighead carp positive control samples and 50 negative control samples. Contamination was not observed in any negative control sample (i.e., DNA was not detected in any laboratory negative control sample or negative PCR control) or in any cooler blank. The DNA of Asian carp was detected in all laboratory positive control samples and positive PCR controls.

The location and the detection of silver carp DNA is reported in Table 2, Figures 1-8 and Appendix 1. Thirty four of the 50 environmental samples below Lock and Dam 19 were considered to be presumptive PCR-positive for the presence of silver carp DNA. Sixteen of 17 of these environmental samples were found to be determinative PCR-positive; all determinative PCR-positive samples were confirmed positive for silver carp DNA by Sanger sequencing (Appendix 3). The DNA extracted from the positive control site (below Lock and Dam 19) appeared to be of a higher quality (cleaner bands) and was visually more similar to the bands observed in extracts from the positive extraction and PCR controls than those observed from the negative control sites or surveillance sites (Appendix 2). Only three environmental samples, two from above the St. Croix Falls Dam and one from Square Lake, were found to be determinative PCR-positive for silver carp DNA. The DNA sequences of the determinative PCR products of these three environmental samples were identified as not being silver carp DNA (Appendix 3). The number of samples processed and the portion of presumptive PCR-positive, determinative PCR-positive and confirmed positive samples in which silver carp DNA was detected are reported in Table 2; results of samples processed to detect bighead carp DNA are reported in Table 3. Results of Sanger sequencing of determinative PCR-positive environmental samples are summarized in Appendix 3.

The location and the detection of bighead carp DNA is reported in Table 3, Figures 1-8 and Appendix 1. Bighead carp DNA was not detected in any of the environmental samples, including those collected below Lock and Dam 19 where bighead carp are often captured by commercial fishers (Iowa Department of Natural Resources, 2012).

Table 2.   Number of presumptive PCR-positive, determinative PCR-positive and confirmed positive (by PCR product sequencing) samples in which the DNA of silver carp was detected.

Site	Sample type	Total # samples	Presumptive PCR-positive	Determinative PCR-positive	Confirmed positives
Positive Control Site					
Below Lock and Dam 19	River water	50	34	16 of 17*	16 of 16*
	Cooler blank	3	0	--	--
Negative Control Sites					
Square Lake	Lake water	50	11	1	0
	Cooler blank	3	0	--	--
Lake Riley	Lake water	50	6	0	--
	Cooler blank	3	0	--	--
Mississippi River Test Sites					
Above Dam at Coon Rapids	River water	50	2	0	--
	Cooler blank	3	0	--	--
Below Dam at Coon Rapids	River water	50	2	0	--
	Cooler blank	3	0	--	--
Below Lock and Dam 1	River water	50	12	0	--
	Cooler blank	3	0	--	--
St. Croix River Test Sites					
Above St. Croix Falls Dam	River water	50	6	2	0
	Cooler blank	3	0	--	--
Below St. Croix Falls Dam	River water	50	10	0	--
	Cooler blank	3	0	--	--
Laboratory Controls					
Negative control	Water	50	0	--	--
Silver carp slurry (positive control)	Slurry	25	25	NA	NA

*The QAPP recommends that 5% of the positives be sampled unless ecologically important. Since the site below Lock and Dam 19 has a population of bighead carp and silver carp that represent a significant portion of the commercial harvest of that water body, it was classified as a positive control. Nonetheless, 50% of the presumptive PCR-positives were re-analyzed and 100% of the amplicons of the determinative PCR-positive samples sequenced.

Table 3.   Number of presumptive PCR-positive, determinative PCR-positive and confirmed positive (by PCR product sequencing) samples in which the DNA of bighead carp was detected.

Site	Sample type	Total # samples	Presumptive PCR-positive	Determinative PCR-positive	Confirmed positives
Positive Control Site					
Below Lock and Dam 19	River water	50	0	--	--
	Cooler blank	3	0	--	--
Negative Control Sites					
Square Lake	Lake water	50	0	--	--
	Cooler blank	3	0	--	--
Lake Riley	Lake water	50	0	--	--
	Cooler blank	3	0	--	--
Mississippi River Test Sites					
Above Dam at Coon Rapids	River water	50	0	--	--
	Cooler blank	3	0	--	--
Below Dam at Coon Rapids	River water	50	0	--	--
	Cooler blank	3	0	--	--
Below Lock and Dam 1	River water	50	1	0	--
	Cooler blank	3	0	--	--
St. Croix River Test Sites					
Above St. Croix Falls Dam	River water	50	0	--	--
	Cooler blank	3	0	--	--
Below St. Croix Falls Dam	River water	50	0	--	--
	Cooler blank	3	0	--	--
Laboratory Controls					
Negative control	Well water	50	0	--	--
Bighead carp slurry (positive control)	Slurry	25	25	NA	NA

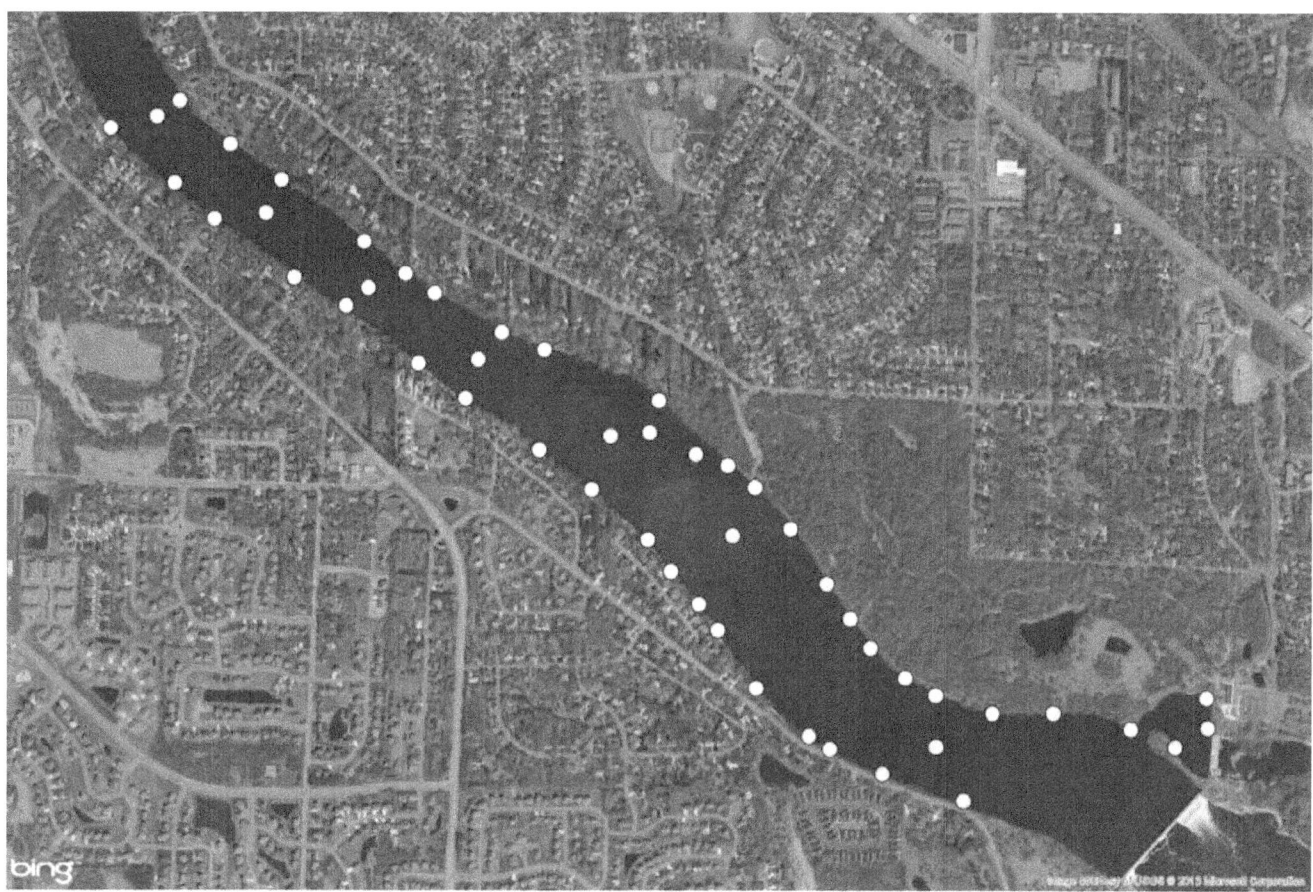

Figure 1.   Detection of silver and bighead carp eDNA above the Coon Rapids Dam (Mississippi River) on September 18, 2012. Sample location of each 2-L water sample; circles indicate that the DNA of silver carp or bighead carp DNA was not detected.

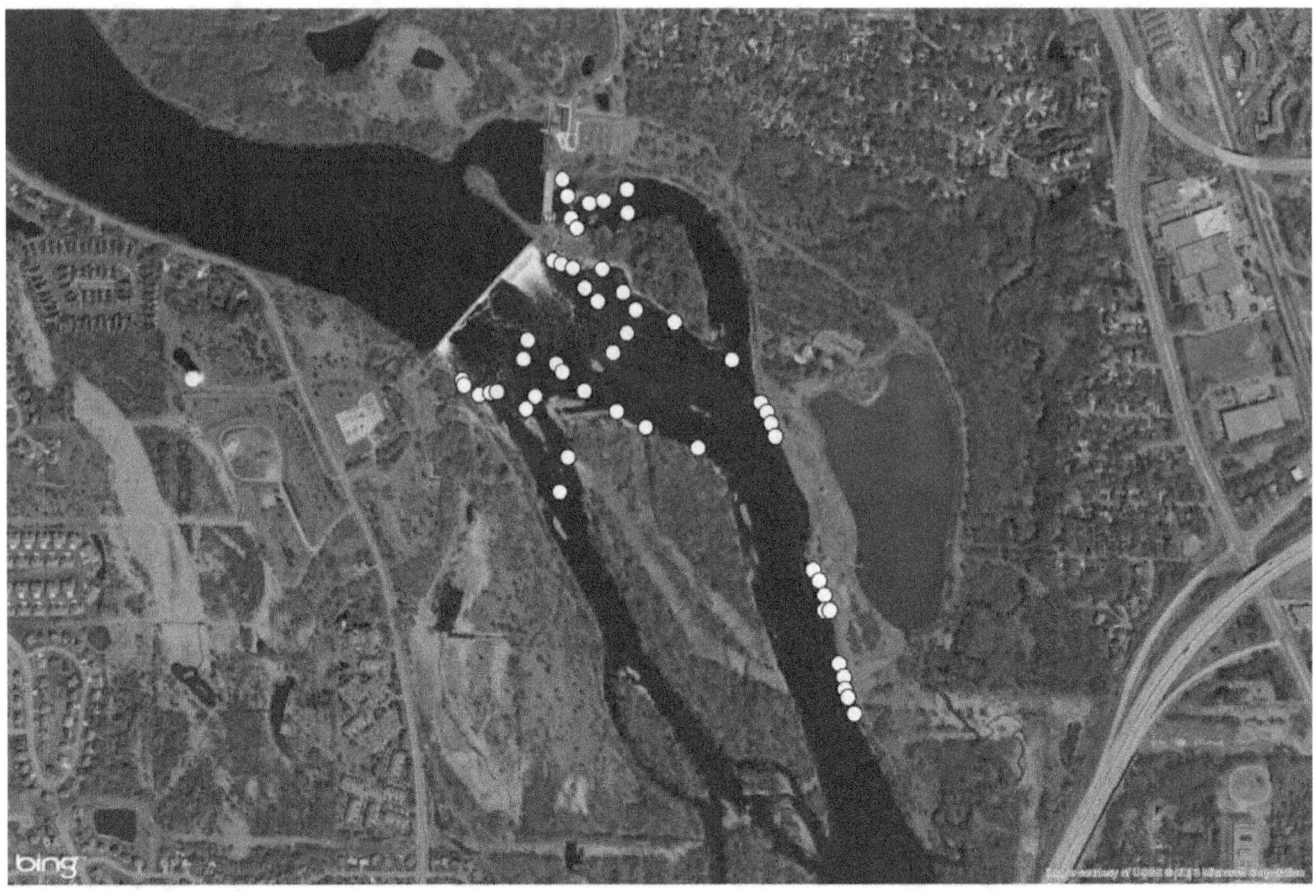

Figure 2.   Detection of silver and bighead carp eDNA below the Coon Rapids Dam (Mississippi River) on September 24, 2012. Sample location of each 2-L water sample; circles indicate that the DNA of silver carp or bighead carp DNA was not detected.

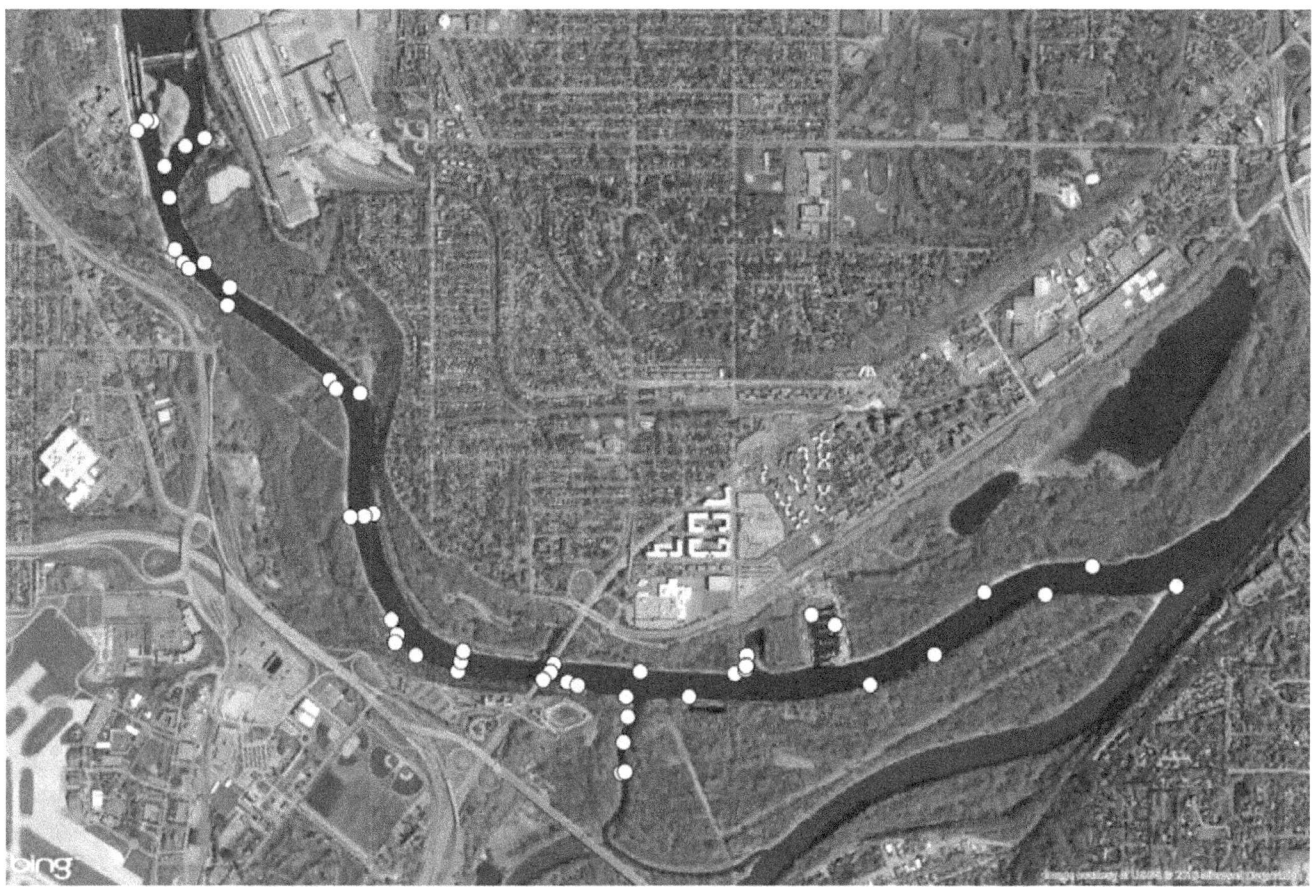

Figure 3. Detection of silver and bighead carp eDNA below Lock and Dam #1 (Mississippi River) on September 25, 2012. Sample location of each 2-L water sample; circles indicate that the DNA of silver carp or bighead carp DNA was not detected.

Figure 4.   Detection of silver and bighead carp eDNA above St. Croix Falls (St. Croix River) on September 17, 2012. Sample location of each 2-L water sample; circles indicate that the DNA of silver carp or bighead carp DNA was not detected.

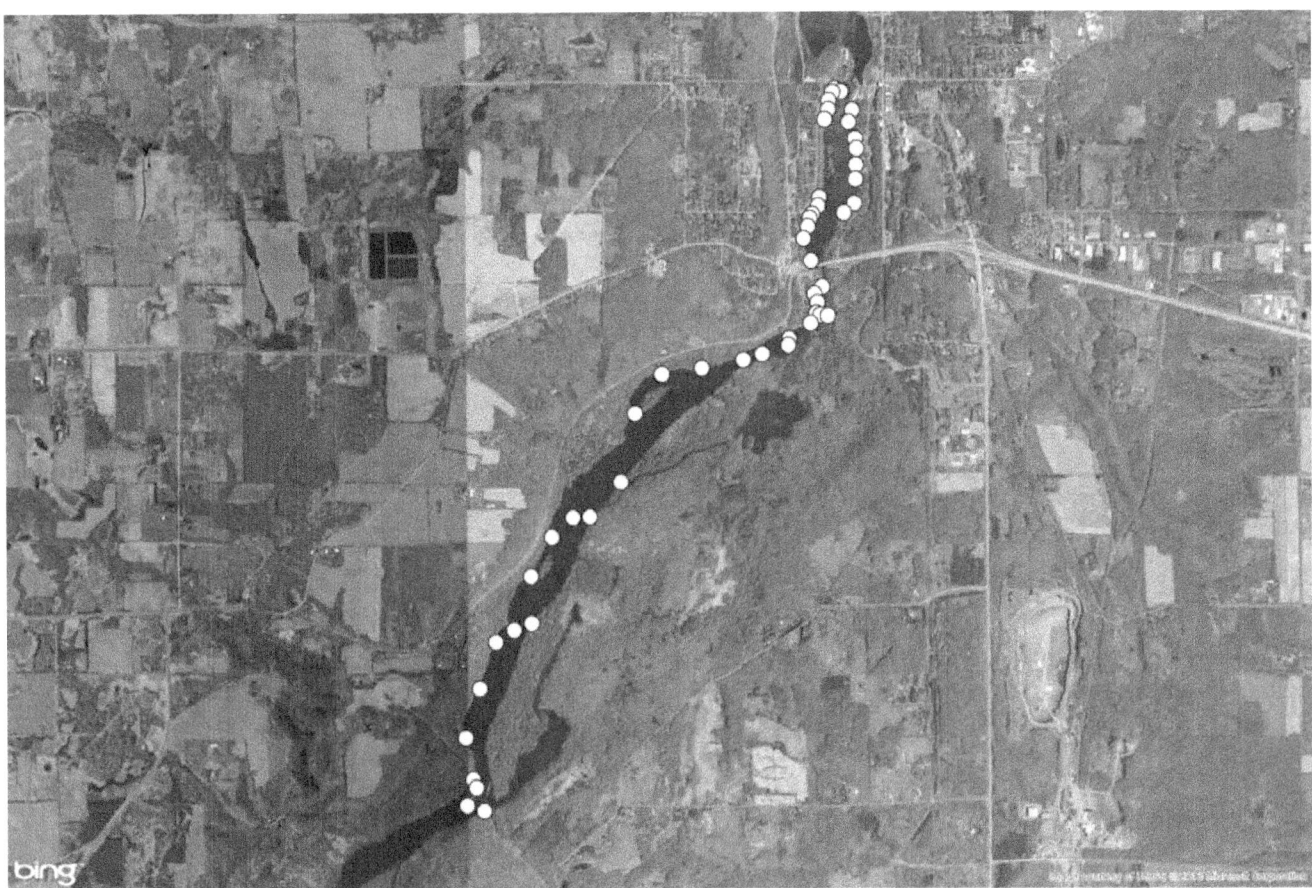

Figure 5.   Detection of silver and bighead carp eDNA below St. Croix Falls (St. Croix River) on September 19, 2012. Sample location of each 2-L water sample; circles indicate that the DNA of silver carp or bighead carp DNA was not detected.

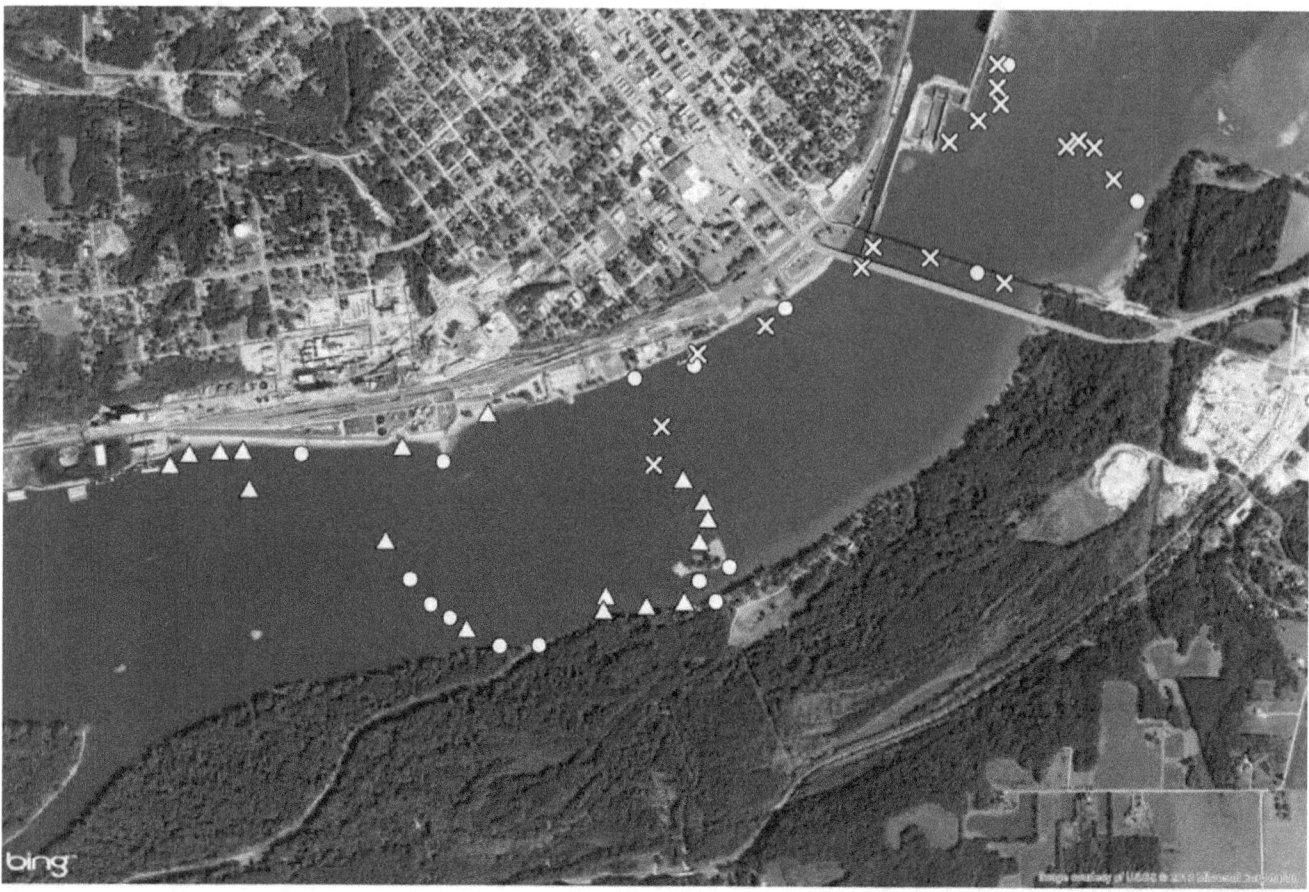

Figure 6.   Detection of silver and bighead carp eDNA below Lock and Dam 19 (Mississippi River) on October 16, 2012. Sample location of each 2-L water sample; circles indicate that silver carp DNA was not detected, "X" indicate presumptive PCR-positive samples that were not processed for determinative PCR or sequencing, triangles indicate samples confirmed positive by sequencing. The DNA of bighead carp was not detected in any of the samples.

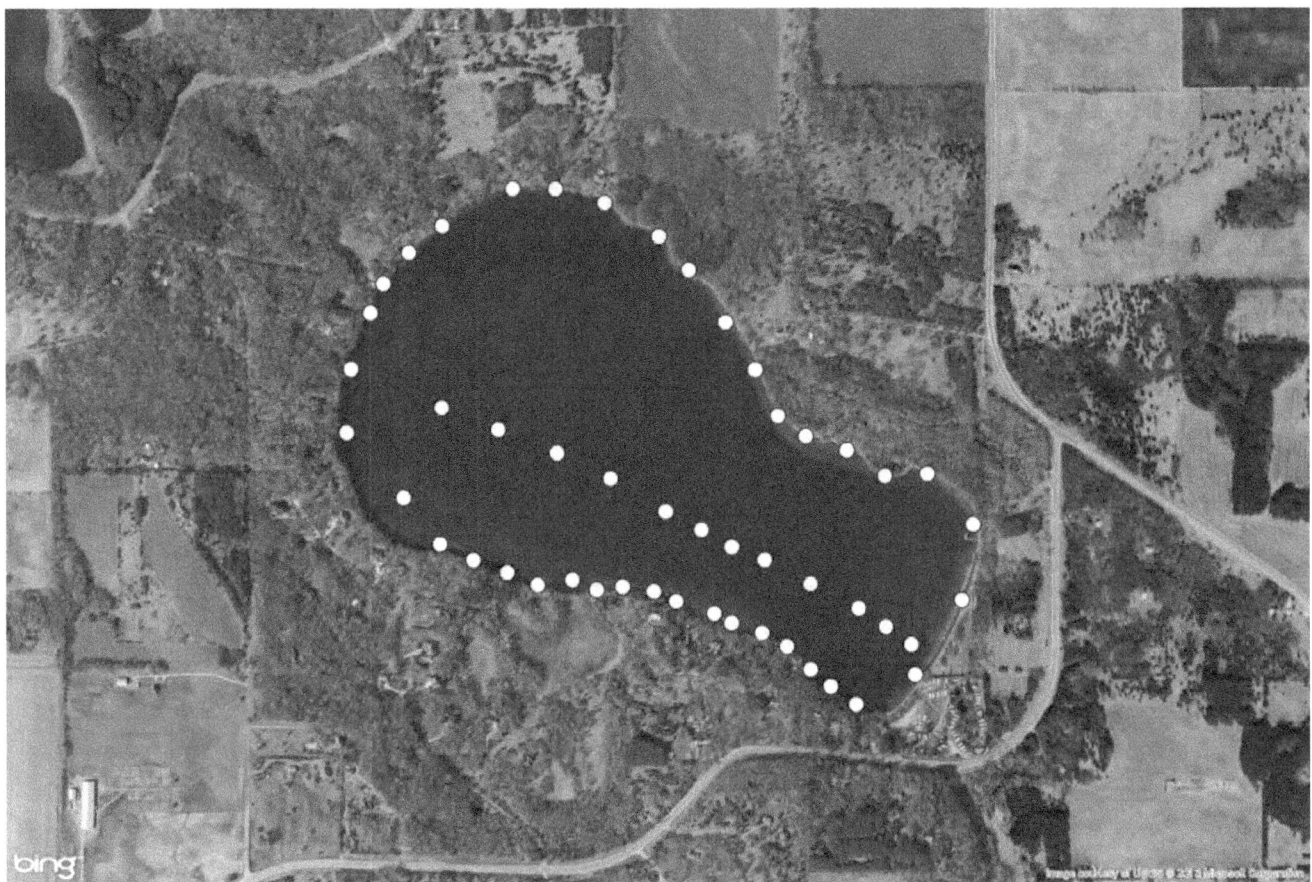

Figure 7. Detection of silver and bighead carp eDNA in Square Lake on October 1, 2012. Sample location of each 2-L water sample; circles indicate that the DNA of silver carp or bighead carp DNA was not detected.

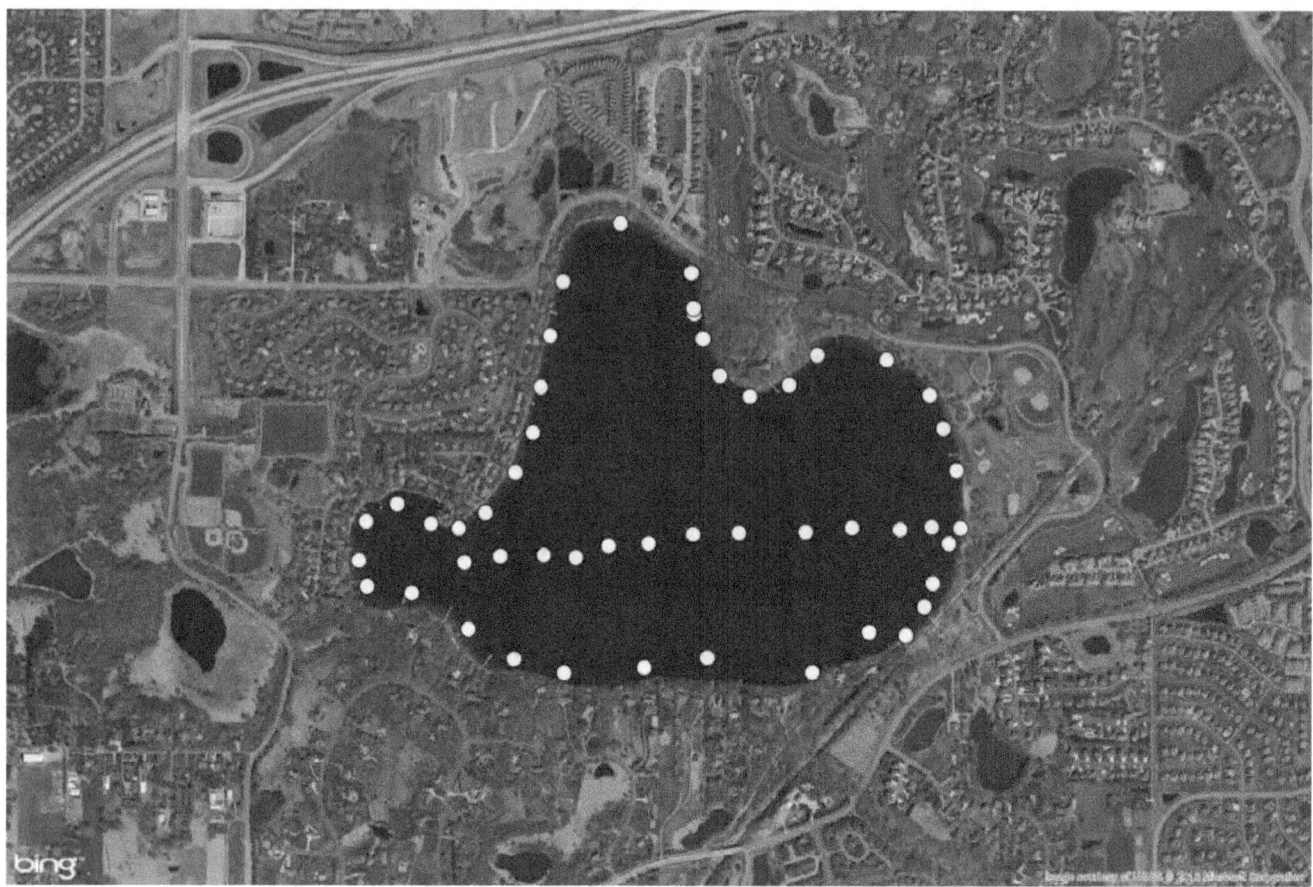

Figure 8.   Detection of silver and bighead carp eDNA in Lake Riley on October 2, 2012. Sample location of each 2-L water sample; circles indicate that the DNA of silver carp or bighead carp DNA was not detected.

Summary

1. The DNA of bighead carp and silver carp was not detected in environmental samples (n=50 per site) collected above and below St. Croix Falls Dam on the St. Croix River, above and below the Coon Rapids Dam and below Lock and Dam 1 on the Mississippi River, and from two negative control lakes, Square Lake and Lake Riley.

2. The DNA of silver carp was detected in environmental samples (n=50) collected below Lock and Dam 19 at Keokuk, Iowa, a reach of the river with high silver carp abundance. Not all samples were presumptive PCR-positive, but the portion (68%) was similar to that reported in the scientific literature for an abundant species (e.g., bighead carp and silver carp, Jerde et al. 2011; common carp *Cyprinus carpio*; Mahon et al. 2013). All determinative PCR-positive samples were confirmed to be silver carp DNA.

3. The DNA of bighead carp was not detected in environmental samples (n=50) collected below Lock and Dam 19, a reach of the river known to have bighead carp.

4. The previous reported detections of the DNA of silver carp in samples collected in 2011 (Hickox et al. 2011; Hsu et al. 2012) were not replicated in this study. Those previous studies used a hybridization technique as a final confirmation that a PCR-positive sample contained silver carp DNA. The USACE QAPP followed here uses sequencing (forward and reverse) to confirm whether the DNA in a PCR-positive sample is/is not the DNA of bighead carp or silver carp.

5. Sequencing (forward and reverse) PCR-positive samples provides the greatest certainty that the DNA of the target species is present and should be used in any location where the target species is thought to be rare or absent (i.e., all locations other than positive control sites). Any monitoring program using current markers for Asian carp (e.g. Jerde et al. 2011) should use sequencing as the final confirmation step to assure comparability of results across years and locations.

Acknowledgements

This project could not have been completed without Byron Karns of the National Park Service, who provided resources, equipment and time for the collection and processing of field water samples. James Lamer of Western Illinois University provided valuable insight, guidance and resources for samples collected below Lock and Dam 19. Finally, this project was funded through reimbursable agreement number 13EMN00000002 with the University of Minnesota, which received financial support from the Environment and Natural Resources Trust Fund.

References

Altschul, SF, TL Madden, AA Schaffer, JH Zhang, Z Zhang, W Miller and DJ Lipman. 1997. Gapped BLAST and PSI-BLAST: a new generation of protein database search programs. Nucleic Acids Research. 25(17): 3389–3402.

Hickox, T, F-C Hsu, R Wong, and T Brito-Robinson. 2011. eDNA Surveillance of Asian Carp on the St. Croix and Mississippi Rivers. Final Report 11 August 2011. Report to the Minnesota Department of Natural Resources, St. Paul.

Hsu, F-C., R Wong, T Brito-Robinson, and M Hayes. 2012. eDNA Surveillance of Asian Carp in Minnesota waters, Fall 2011. Report to the Minnesota Department of Natural Resources, St. Paul.

Iowa Department of Natural Resources. 2012. Commercial Fish Report for Iowa Boundary Waters of the Mississippi and Missouri Rivers.

Jerde, CL, AR Mahon, WL Chadderton, and DM Lodge. 2011. 'Sight-Unseen' Detection of Rare Aquatic Species Using Environmental DNA. Conservation Letters. 4: 150–157. DOI: 10.1111/j.1755-263X.2010.00158.x.

Mahon, AR, CL Jerde, M Galaska, JL Bergner, WL Chadderton, DM. Lodge, ME Hunter, LG Nico. 2013. Validation of eDNA Surveillance Sensitivity for Detection of Asian Carps in Controlled and Field Experiments. PLoS ONE 8(3): e58316. doi:10.1371/journal.pone.0058316

U.S. Army Corps of Engineers. 2012. Quality Assurance Project Plan: eDNA Monitoring of Invasive Asian Carp in the Chicago Area Waterway System. Retrieved from *http://www.asiancarp.us/documents/USACE-eDNA-QAPP.pdf*

U.S. Army Corps of Engineers. 2013. Environmental DNA Calibration Study: Interim Technical Review Report. Retrieved from *http://www.asiancarp.us/documents/ECALS_INTERIM.pdf*

U.S. Geological Survey. 2013. Nonindigenous Aquatic Species Database. Available from: *http://nas.er.usgs.gov. Accessed 05 March 2013.*

Appendixes 1–3

Appendix 1.   Sample number, location of environmental sample collection, whether the sample was a cooler blank or filter positive control and notes on the presence of avian predators for each site. Additionally, the number of presumptive PCR-positives of the 8 PCR per sample, number of determinative PCR-positives of the 8 PCR per presumptive-positive sample and if the sample was confirmed positive for silver carp and/or bighead carp DNA.

Appendix 2.   Representative electrophoresis gels for the detection of the DNA of silver carp in samples taken from each site. Gels used for the detection of bighead carp were not included because bighead carp DNA was not detected. Representative gels for presumptive and determinative PCR-positives are included.

Appendix 3.   Sequences of determinative PCR-positive environmental samples amplified with the silver carp marker. The percent match of each sequence to published silver carp DNA sequences in GenBank (*http://www.ncbi.nlm.nih.gov/genbank/*) is included following the sequence. A sample was determined "confirmed positive" only when both the forward and reverse sequences of that sample were greater than 95% similar to published silver carp sequences.

Appendix 1.   Sample number, location of environmental sample collection, whether the sample was a cooler blank or filter positive control and notes on the presence of avian predators for each site. Additionally, the number of presumptive PCR-positives of the 8 PCR per sample, number of determinative PCR-positives of the 8 PCR per presumptive-positive sample and if the sample was confirmed positive for silver carp and/or bighead carp DNA.

Date collected: September 17, 2012 Location: St. Croix River above St. Croix Falls Dam					Silver Carp			Bighead Carp			
ID	Easting	Northing	Blank	No. of Filters	Presumptive PCR-Positives	Determinative PCR-Positives	Confirmed	Presumptive PCR-Positives	Determinative PCR-Positives	Confirmed	NOTES
001	0525454	5034558	-----	2	0	0	-----	0	0	-----	eagle eating fish nearby
002	0525463	5034485	-----	2	0	0	-----	0	0	-----	eagle eating fish nearby
003	0525426	5034375	-----	2	0	0	-----	0	0	-----	osprey flew over
004	0525378	5034242	-----	2	0	0	-----	0	0	-----	
005	0525584	5034178	-----	2	1	0	-----	0	0	-----	
006	0525746	5034269	-----	2	0	0	-----	0	0	-----	
007	0525905	5034279	BLANK	2	0	0	-----	0	0	-----	
008	0525905	5034279	-----	2	0	0	-----	0	0	-----	
009	0525900	5034183	-----	2	0	0	-----	0	0	-----	
010	0525874	5034037	-----	2	2	0	-----	0	0	-----	gull flew over
011	0526335	5033892	-----	2	0	0	-----	0	0	-----	
012	0526499	5034027	-----	2	0	0	-----	0	0	-----	
013	0526994	5033806	-----	2	0	0	-----	0	0	-----	
014	0526974	5033688	-----	2	0	0	-----	0	0	-----	
015	0526980	5033565	-----	2	0	0	-----	0	0	-----	
016	0527222	5032983	-----	2	1	1	NO	0	0	-----	
017	0527495	5032869	-----	2	0	0	-----	0	0	-----	
018	0527611	5032523	-----	2	0	0	-----	0	0	-----	
019	0527533	5032439	-----	2	0	0	-----	0	0	-----	
020	0527500	5032240	-----	2	1	0	-----	0	0	-----	
021	0527551	5031947	-----	2	0	0	-----	0	0	-----	eagle flying nearby
022	0527736	5031932	-----	2	0	0	-----	0	0	-----	
023	0527781	5031704	-----	2	0	0	-----	0	0	-----	
024	0527680	5031676	-----	2	0	0	-----	0	0	-----	
025	0527571	5031702	-----	2	0	0	-----	0	0	-----	
026	0527537	5031489	-----	2	0	0	-----	0	0	-----	
027	0527444	5031355	-----	2	0	0	-----	0	0	-----	
028	0527638	5031285	-----	2	0	0	-----	0	0	-----	
029	0527599	5030986	-----	2	0	0	-----	0	0	-----	kingfisher
030	0527503	5030989	-----	2	0	0	-----	0	0	-----	
031	0527371	5030977	-----	2	0	0	-----	0	0	-----	
032	0527345	5030823	-----	2	0	0	-----	0	0	-----	
033	0527585	5030737	-----	2	0	0	-----	0	0	-----	
034	0527603	5030613	-----	2	0	0	-----	0	0	-----	
035	0527503	5030557	-----	2	0	0	-----	0	0	-----	
036	0527377	5030423	-----	2	0	0	-----	0	0	-----	
037	0527368	5030274	-----	2	0	0	-----	0	0	-----	
038	0527489	5030104	-----	2	0	0	-----	0	0	-----	
039	0527547	5029975	-----	2	0	0	-----	0	0	-----	cormorant
040	0527398	5029906	BLANK	1	0	0	-----	0	0	-----	
041	0527398	5029906	-----	2	0	0	-----	0	0	-----	
042	0527240	5029786	-----	2	0	0	-----	0	0	-----	
043	0527235	5029717	-----	2	1	1	NO	0	0	-----	
044	0527483	5029660	-----	2	0	0	-----	0	0	-----	
045	0527498	5029616	-----	2	0	0	-----	0	0	-----	
046	0527498	5029450	-----	2	0	0	-----	0	0	-----	
047	0527413	5029397	-----	2	0	0	-----	0	0	-----	
048	0527272	5029356	BLANK	1	0	0	-----	0	0	-----	
049	0527272	5029356	-----	2	0	0	-----	0	0	-----	
050	0527280	5029283	-----	2	0	0	-----	0	0	-----	
051	0527256	5029134	-----	2	0	0	-----	0	0	-----	
052	0527339	5028935	-----	2	0	0	-----	0	0	-----	
053	0527475	5028017	-----	2	3	0	-----	0	0	-----	
054	-----	-----	Filter +	2	3	-----	-----	-----	-----	-----	

Date collected: September 18, 2012 Location: Mississippi River Above Coon Rapids Dam					Silver Carp			Bighead Carp			
ID	Easting	Northing	Blank	No. of Filters	Presumptive PCR-Positives	Determinative PCR-Positives	Confirmed	Presumptive PCR-Positives	Determinative PCR-Positives	Confirmed	NOTES
001	472878	5000841	-----	2	1	0	-----	0	0	-----	
002	473012	5000730	-----	2	0	0	-----	0	0	-----	
003	473146	5000639	-----	2	0	0	-----	0	0	-----	
004	473368	5000482	-----	3	0	0	-----	0	0	-----	
005	473479	5000400	-----	2	0	0	-----	0	0	-----	
006	472818	5000802	-----	2	0	0	-----	0	0	-----	
007	473106	5000555	-----	2	0	0	-----	0	0	-----	
008	473379	5000364	-----	2	0	0	-----	0	0	-----	
009	472695	5000771	-----	2	0	0	-----	0	0	-----	
010	472864	5000631	-----	2	0	0	-----	0	0	-----	
011	472970	5000540	-----	2	0	0	-----	0	0	-----	
012	473181	5000390	BLANK	1	0	0	-----	0	0	-----	
013	473181	5000390	-----	2	0	0	-----	0	0	-----	
014	473320	5000318	-----	2	0	0	-----	0	0	-----	
015	473514	5000172	-----	2	0	0	-----	0	0	-----	
016	473639	5000083	-----	2	2	0	-----	0	0	-----	
017	473835	4999951	-----	2	0	0	-----	0	0	-----	
018	473973	4999850	-----	2	0	0	-----	0	0	-----	
019	474120	4999722	-----	2	0	0	-----	0	0	-----	
020	473673	5000182	-----	2	0	0	-----	0	0	-----	
021	474023	4999986	-----	2	0	0	-----	0	0	-----	
022	473557	5000350	-----	2	0	0	-----	0	0	-----	
023	473736	5000250	-----	2	0	0	-----	0	0	-----	
024	473848	5000206	-----	2	0	0	-----	0	0	-----	
025	474150	5000077	BLANK	1	0	0	-----	0	0	-----	
026	474150	5000077	-----	2	0	0	-----	0	0	-----	
027	474334	4999911	-----	2	0	0	-----	0	0	-----	eagle flying nearby
028	474405	4999855	-----	2	0	0	-----	0	0	-----	
029	474501	4999749	-----	2	0	0	-----	0	0	-----	
030	474599	4999609	-----	2	0	0	-----	0	0	-----	
031	474662	4999520	-----	2	0	0	-----	0	0	-----	
032	474716	4999446	-----	2	0	0	-----	0	0	-----	
033	474347	4999732	-----	2	0	0	-----	0	0	-----	
034	474182	4999641	-----	2	0	0	-----	0	0	-----	
035	474257	4999557	-----	4	0	0	-----	0	0	-----	
036	474308	4999492	-----	2	0	0	-----	0	0	-----	
037	474408	4999343	-----	2	0	0	-----	0	0	-----	
038	474552	4999221	-----	2	0	0	-----	0	0	-----	
039	474608	4999188	-----	2	0	0	-----	0	0	-----	
040	474749	4999125	-----	4	0	0	-----	0	0	-----	
041	474966	4999057	-----	2	0	0	-----	0	0	-----	
042	474125	4999995	-----	2	0	0	-----	0	0	-----	
043	474249	4999939	-----	2	0	0	-----	0	0	-----	
044	474893	4999194	BLANK	1	0	0	-----	0	0	-----	
045	474893	4999194	-----	2	0	0	-----	0	0	-----	
046	474812	4999369	-----	2	0	0	-----	0	0	-----	
047	474892	4999325	-----	2	0	0	-----	0	0	-----	
048	475044	4999279	-----	2	0	0	-----	0	0	-----	
049	475209	4999280	-----	2	0	0	-----	0	0	-----	
050	475415	4999239	-----	2	0	0	-----	0	0	-----	
051	475535	4999194	-----	2	0	0	-----	0	0	-----	gull over dam
052	475619	4999319	-----	2	0	0	-----	0	0	-----	
053	475622	4999243	-----	2	0	0	-----	0	0	-----	
054	-----	-----	Filter +	2	5	-----	-----	-----	-----	-----	

| Date collected: September 19, 2012
Location: St. Croix River below St. Croix Falls Dam | | | | | Silver Carp | | | Bighead Carp | | | |
ID	Easting	Northing	Blank	No. of Filters	Presumptive PCR-Positives	Determinative PCR-Positives	Confirmed	Presumptive PCR-Positives	Determinative PCR-Positives	Confirmed	NOTES
001	0527473	5028738	-----	2	1	0	-----	0	0	-----	
002	0527523	5028725	-----	2	0	0	-----	0	0	-----	
003	0527512	5028722	-----	2	2	0	-----	0	0	-----	
004	0527459	5028717	BLANK	2	0	0	-----	0	0	-----	many crows above
005	0527459	5028717	-----	2	1	0	-----	0	0	-----	
006	0527434	5028668	-----	2	0	0	-----	0	0	-----	
007	0527432	5028613	-----	2	1	0	-----	0	0	-----	
008	0527409	5028552	-----	2	0	0	-----	0	0	-----	
009	0527373	5028074	-----	2	0	0	-----	0	0	-----	eagle
010	0527365	5028020	-----	2	2	0	-----	0	0	-----	
011	0527320	5027686	-----	1	0	0	-----	0	0	-----	
012	0527328	5027969	-----	2	0	0	-----	0	0	-----	
013	0527311	5027945	-----	2	2	0	-----	0	0	-----	
014	0527298	5027895	-----	2	0	0	-----	0	0	-----	
015	0527271	5027822	-----	2	0	0	-----	0	0	-----	
016	0527585	5028608	-----	3	0	0	-----	0	0	-----	crows above, feces
017	0527562	5028535	-----	2	1	0	-----	0	0	-----	
018	0527606	5028431	-----	2	1	0	-----	0	0	-----	
019	0527614	5028370	-----	2	0	0	-----	0	0	-----	
020	0527610	5028271	-----	2	0	0	-----	0	0	-----	
021	0527599	5028037	-----	2	0	0	-----	0	0	-----	
022	0527532	5027979	-----	2	0	0	-----	0	0	-----	
023	0527608	5028184	-----	2	0	0	-----	0	0	-----	
024	0527390	5027526	-----	2	0	0	-----	0	0	-----	
025	0527342	5027481	-----	2	0	0	-----	0	0	-----	
026	0527360	5027428	-----	2	0	0	-----	0	0	-----	
027	0527352	5027362	-----	2	0	0	-----	0	0	-----	
028	0527378	5027352	-----	2	0	0	-----	0	0	-----	
029	0527427	5027348	-----	2	0	0	-----	0	0	-----	
030	0527316	5027301	-----	2	0	0	-----	0	0	-----	
031	0527174	5027206	-----	2	0	0	-----	0	0	-----	
032	0527169	5027167	-----	2	0	0	-----	0	0	-----	
033	0527000	5027114	-----	2	0	0	-----	0	0	-----	
034	0526882	5027080	-----	2	0	0	-----	0	0	-----	
035	0526619	5027030	BLANK	1	0	0	-----	0	0	-----	
036	0526619	5027030	-----	2	0	0	-----	0	0	-----	
037	0526365	5026992	-----	2	0	0	-----	0	0	-----	turkey vulture
038	0526196	5026750	-----	2	0	0	-----	0	0	-----	
039	0526103	5026332	-----	2	0	0	-----	0	0	-----	
040	0525905	5026121	-----	2	0	0	-----	0	0	-----	
041	0525798	5026117	-----	2	1	0	-----	0	0	-----	
042	0525661	5025997	-----	2	0	0	-----	0	0	-----	
043	0525526	5025755	-----	2	0	0	-----	0	0	-----	
044	0525530	5025469	-----	2	0	0	-----	0	0	-----	
045	0525420	5025428	-----	2	0	0	-----	0	0	-----	
046	0525301	5025355	-----	2	0	0	-----	0	0	-----	
047	0525196	5025069	-----	2	0	0	-----	0	0	-----	
048	0525104	5024767	-----	2	0	0	-----	0	0	-----	
049	0525151	5024513	-----	2	0	0	-----	0	0	-----	
050	0525172	5024463	-----	2	0	0	-----	0	0	-----	
051	0525223	5024321	BLANK	1	0	0	-----	0	0	-----	
052	0525223	5024321	-----	2	0	0	-----	0	0	-----	
053	0525113	5024353	-----	2	1	0	-----	0	0	-----	
054	-----	-----	Filter +	2	0	-----	-----	-----	-----	-----	

Date collected: September 24, 2012 Location: Mississippi River below Coon Rapids Dam					Silver Carp			Bighead Carp			
ID	Easting	Northing	Blank	No. of Filters	Presumptive PCR-Positives	Determinative PCR-Positives	Confirmed	Presumptive PCR-Positives	Determinative PCR-Positives	Confirmed	NOTES
001	475672	4999208	-----	2	0	0	-----	0	0	-----	
002	475683	4999174	-----	2	0	0	-----	0	0	-----	
003	475691	4999129	-----	2	0	0	-----	0	0	-----	
004	475730	4999160	-----	2	0	0	-----	0	0	-----	
005	475761	4999165	-----	2	0	0	-----	0	0	-----	
006	475811	4999188	-----	2	0	0	-----	0	0	-----	
007	475703	4999109	-----	2	0	0	-----	0	0	-----	
008	475651	4999042	-----	4	0	0	-----	0	0	-----	
009	475669	4999035	-----	4	0	0	-----	0	0	-----	
010	475694	4999027	-----	6	0	0	-----	0	0	-----	
011	475720	4998986	-----	2	0	0	-----	0	0	-----	
012	475748	4998959	-----	2	0	0	-----	0	0	-----	
013	475757	4999025	-----	4	1	0	-----	0	0	-----	
014	475802	4998977	-----	2	1	0	-----	0	0	-----	
015	475829	4998941	-----	2	0	0	-----	0	0	-----	eagle flying
016	475810	4998894	-----	2	0	0	-----	0	0	-----	
167	475780	4998854	-----	2	0	0	-----	0	0	-----	
168	475914	4998916	-----	2	0	0	-----	0	0	-----	
019	476035	4998838	-----	2	0	0	-----	0	0	-----	
020	475812	4999140	BLANK	2	0	0	-----	0	0	-----	
021	475812	4999140	-----	2	0	0	-----	0	0	-----	
022	475455	4998797	-----	2	0	0	-----	0	0	-----	
023	475459	4998787	-----	2	0	0	-----	0	0	-----	
024	475492	4998767	-----	2	0	0	-----	0	0	-----	
025	475516	4998772	-----	2	0	0	-----	0	0	-----	
026	475530	4998774	-----	2	0	0	-----	0	0	-----	
027	475591	4998738	-----	2	0	0	-----	0	0	-----	
028	475611	4998764	-----	2	0	0	-----	0	0	-----	
029	476098	4998751	-----	2	0	0	-----	0	0	-----	
030	475658	4998831	-----	2	0	0	-----	0	0	-----	about 100 gulls
031	475671	4998814	-----	2	0	0	-----	0	0	-----	about 100 gulls
032	475595	4998879	BLANK	1	0	0	-----	0	0	-----	
033	475595	4998879	-----	2	0	0	-----	0	0	-----	
034	475586	4998840	-----	4	0	0	-----	0	0	-----	
035	475719	4998775	-----	2	0	0	-----	0	0	-----	
036	475788	4998733	-----	2	0	0	-----	0	0	-----	
037	475851	4998700	-----	2	0	0	-----	0	0	-----	
038	475963	4998657	-----	2	0	0	-----	0	0	-----	
039	475665	4998568	-----	2	0	0	-----	0	0	-----	
040	475683	4998639	-----	2	0	0	-----	0	0	-----	
041	476111	4998731	-----	4	0	0	-----	0	0	-----	
042	476120	4998708	-----	2	0	0	-----	0	0	-----	
043	476129	4998681	-----	2	0	0	-----	0	0	-----	
044	476209	4998407	-----	2	0	0	-----	0	0	-----	
045	476222	4998385	-----	2	0	0	-----	0	0	-----	
046	476233	4998355	BLANK	1	0	0	-----	0	0	-----	
047	476233	4998324	-----	2	0	0	-----	0	0	-----	
048	476244	4998324	-----	2	0	0	-----	0	0	-----	
049	476263	4998215	-----	6	0	0	-----	0	0	-----	
050	476274	4998188	-----	2	0	0	-----	0	0	-----	
051	476276	4998162	-----	2	0	0	-----	0	0	-----	
052	476282	4998145	-----	6	0	0	-----	0	0	-----	
053	476296	4998112	-----	6	0	0	-----	0	0	-----	
054	Not collected										

Date collected: September 25, 2012 Location: Mississippi River below Lock and Dam 1					Silver Carp			Bighead Carp			
ID	Easting	Northing	Blank	No. of Filters	Presumptive PCR-Positives	Determinative PCR-Positives	Confirmed	Presumptive PCR-Positives	Determinative PCR-Positives	Confirmed	NOTES
001	484088	4973332	-----	2	1	0	-----	0	0	-----	
002	484063	4973334	-----	2	0	0	-----	0	0	-----	
003	484027	4973295	-----	2	0	0	-----	0	0	-----	gull flew over
004	484137	4973159	-----	2	1	0	-----	0	0	-----	
005	484221	4973235	-----	2	0	0	-----	0	0	-----	gull over island
006	484299	4973267	-----	2	0	0	-----	0	0	-----	
007	484157	4973038	-----	2	0	0	-----	0	0	-----	
008	484180	4972841	BLANK	1	0	0	-----	0	0	-----	
009	484180	4972841	-----	2	0	0	-----	0	0	-----	gull
010	484214	4972790	-----	2	0	0	-----	0	0	-----	
011	484235	4972767	-----	2	0	0	-----	0	0	-----	
012	484297	4972789	-----	2	0	0	-----	0	0	-----	eagle flying over
013	484397	4972694	-----	2	0	0	-----	0	0	-----	
014	484388	4972626	-----	2	0	0	-----	0	0	-----	
015	484794	4972340	-----	2	0	0	-----	0	0	-----	
016	484819	4972306	-----	2	0	0	-----	0	0	-----	
017	484916	4972291	-----	2	0	0	-----	0	0	-----	
018	484968	4971827	-----	2	0	0	-----	0	0	-----	
019	484931	4971818	-----	2	0	0	-----	0	0	-----	
020	484875	4971816	-----	2	0	0	-----	0	0	-----	
021	485039	4971421	-----	4	1	0	-----	0	0	-----	
022	485064	4971364	-----	2	0	0	-----	0	0	-----	
023	485054	4971332	-----	2	0	0	-----	0	0	-----	
024	485138	4971285	-----	2	0	0	-----	0	0	-----	
025	485306	4971223	-----	2	1	0	-----	0	0	-----	
026	485319	4971261	-----	2	0	0	-----	0	0	-----	
027	485327	4971300	-----	2	0	0	-----	0	0	-----	
028	485691	4971250	-----	2	0	0	-----	0	0	-----	
029	485677	4971219	-----	2	1	0	-----	0	0	-----	
030	485647	4971190	-----	2	0	0	-----	0	0	-----	
031	485745	4971181	-----	2	0	0	-----	0	0	-----	
032	485785	4971168	-----	2	0	0	-----	0	0	-----	
033	485976	4971124	-----	2	0	0	-----	0	0	-----	
034	485983	4971047	-----	2	0	0	-----	0	0	-----	
035	485966	4970950	-----	2	0	0	-----	0	0	-----	
036	485957	4970833	BLANK	1	0	0	-----	0	0	-----	
037	485957	4970833	-----	2	0	0	-----	0	0	-----	
038	485973	4970837	-----	2	0	0	-----	0	0	-----	
039	486032	4971221	-----	2	0	0	-----	0	0	-----	
040	486225	4971124	-----	2	0	0	-----	0	0	-----	
041	486409	4971214	-----	2	4	0	-----	1	0		
042	486453	4971230	-----	2	0	0	-----	0	0	-----	
043	486456	4971284	-----	4	0	0	-----	0	0	-----	
044	486454	4971243	-----	2	0	0	-----	0	0	-----	
045	486717	4971439	-----	2	0	0	-----	0	0	-----	
046	486812	4971400	-----	2	2	0	-----	0	0	-----	
047	486954	4971170	-----	2	4	0	-----	0	0	-----	
048	487216	4971287	-----	2	0	0	-----	0	0	-----	
049	487664	4971517	BLANK	1	0	0	-----	0	0	-----	
050	487664	4971517	-----	2	3	0	-----	0	0	-----	
051	488189	4971550	-----	2	2	0	-----	0	0	-----	
052	487851	4971625	-----	2	4	0	-----	0	0	-----	
053	487416	4971526	-----	2	2	0	-----	0	0	-----	
054	-----	-----	Filter +	3	8	-----	-----	-----	-----	-----	

Date collected: October 1, 2012 Location: Square Lake					Silver Carp			Bighead Carp			
ID	Easting	Northing	Blank	No. of Filters	Presumptive PCR-Positives	Determinative PCR-Positives	Confirmed	Presumptive PCR-Positives	Determinative PCR-Positives	Confirmed	NOTES
001	0515976	4999913	-----	2	0	0	-----	0	0	-----	
002	0515846	4999852	-----	1	0	0	-----	0	0	-----	
003	0515792	4999889	-----	1	0	0	-----	0	0	-----	
004	0515749	4999924	-----	1	1	0	-----	0	0	-----	
005	0515697	4999971	-----	2	0	0	-----	0	0	-----	
006	0515644	4999999	-----	1	0	0	-----	0	0	-----	
007	0515580	5000019	-----	1	0	0	-----	0	0	-----	
008	0515544	5000039	-----	1	0	0	-----	0	0	-----	
009	0515463	5000064	-----	1	0	0	-----	0	0	-----	
010	0515416	5000084	-----	2	0	0	-----	0	0	-----	
011	0515350	5000094	-----	1	0	0	-----	0	0	-----	
012	0515295	5000088	-----	1	0	0	-----	0	0	-----	
013	0515243	5000108	-----	1	1	0	-----	0	0	-----	
014	0515168	5000097	-----	1	1	0	-----	0	0	-----	
015	0515103	5000123	-----	1	1	0	-----	0	0	-----	
016	0515030	5000149	-----	1	0	0	-----	0	0	-----	
017	0514959	5000181	BLANK	1	0	0	-----	0	0	-----	
018	0514959	5000181	-----	1	0	0	-----	0	0	-----	
019	0514881	5000277	-----	1	0	0	-----	0	0	-----	
020	0514760	5000410	-----	1	0	0	-----	0	0	-----	
021	0514769	5000541	-----	1	0	0	-----	0	0	-----	
022	0514811	5000655	-----	1	0	0	-----	0	0	-----	
023	0514839	5000715	-----	1	0	0	-----	0	0	-----	
024	0514894	5000779	-----	1	0	0	-----	0	0	-----	
025	0514965	5000834	-----	1	0	0	-----	0	0	-----	
026	0515117	5000910	-----	1	0	0	-----	0	0	-----	
027	0515208	5000909	-----	1	0	0	-----	0	0	-----	
028	0515314	5000881	BLANK	1	0	0	-----	0	0	-----	
029	0515314	5000881	-----	1	0	0	-----	0	0	-----	
030	0515428	5000812	-----	2	0	0	-----	0	0	-----	
031	0515491	5000743	-----	1	0	0	-----	0	0	-----	kingfisher
032	0515569	5000636	-----	2	0	0	-----	0	0	-----	
033	0515631	5000539	-----	1	0	0	-----	0	0	-----	
034	0515679	5000443	-----	1	0	0	-----	0	0	-----	
035	0515739	5000402	-----	1	0	0	-----	0	0	-----	
036	0515827	5000373	-----	1	1	0	-----	0	0	-----	
037	0515910	5000321	-----	1	0	0	-----	0	0	-----	
038	0516003	5000325	-----	1	0	0	-----	0	0	-----	
039	0516100	5000221	-----	1	0	0	-----	0	0	-----	
040	0516076	5000066	-----	1	0	0	-----	0	0	-----	
041	0515968	4999975	-----	1	0	0	-----	0	0	-----	
042	0515912	5000012	-----	1	2	0	-----	0	0	-----	
043	0515852	5000049	-----	1	0	0	-----	0	0	-----	
044	0515749	5000099	-----	1	1	0	-----	0	0	-----	
045	0515650	5000149	BLANK	1	0	0	-----	0	0	-----	
046	0515650	5000149	-----	1	2	0	-----	0	0	-----	
047	0515581	5000175	-----	1	3	0	-----	0	0	-----	
048	0515517	5000211	-----	1	0	0	-----	0	0	-----	
049	0515441	5000248	-----	1	0	0	-----	0	0	-----	
050	0515325	5000315	-----	1	3	0	-----	0	0	-----	
051	0515210	5000368	-----	1	0	0	-----	0	0	-----	
052	0515084	5000416	-----	1	2	1	NO	0	0	-----	
053	0514963	5000461	-----	1	0	0	-----	0	0	-----	
054	-----	-----	Filter +	1	8	-----	-----	-----	-----	-----	

Date collected: October 2, 2012 Location: Lake Riley					Silver Carp			Bighead Carp			
ID	Easting	Northing	Blank	No. of Filters	Presumptive PCR-Positives	Determinative PCR-Positives	Confirmed	Presumptive PCR-Positives	Determinative PCR-Positives	Confirmed	NOTES
001	0459498	4964912	-----	2	0	0	-----	0	0	-----	hawk
002	0459462	4965020	-----	2	0	0	-----	0	0	-----	
003	0459425	4965106	-----	2	0	0	-----	0	0	-----	
004	0459310	4965196	-----	2	0	0	-----	0	0	-----	
005	0459123	4965208	-----	2	0	0	-----	0	0	-----	
006	0459049	4965131	-----	2	0	0	-----	0	0	-----	
007	0458946	4965102	-----	2	0	0	-----	0	0	-----	
008	0458865	4965154	-----	2	0	0	-----	0	0	-----	
009	0458821	4965248	-----	2	0	0	-----	0	0	-----	
010	0458798	4965313	-----	2	0	0	-----	0	0	-----	
011	0458797	4965326	-----	2	0	0	-----	0	0	-----	
012	0458791	4965417	-----	2	0	0	-----	0	0	-----	
013	0458600	4965544	-----	2	0	0	-----	0	0	-----	
014	0458445	4965394	BLANK	1	0	0	-----	0	0	-----	
015	0458445	4965394	-----	2	0	0	-----	0	0	-----	
016	0458410	4965256	-----	2	0	0	-----	0	0	-----	
017	0458384	4965125	-----	2	1	0	-----	0	0	-----	
018	0458362	4965007	-----	2	0	0	-----	0	0	-----	
019	0458316	4964905	-----	2	0	0	-----	0	0	-----	
020	0458236	4964802	-----	2	0	0	-----	0	0	-----	
021	0458163	4964762	-----	2	0	0	-----	0	0	-----	
022	0458085	4964774	-----	2	0	0	-----	0	0	-----	
023	0457995	4964825	-----	2	0	0	-----	0	0	-----	
024	0457912	4964780	-----	2	1	0	-----	0	0	-----	
025	0457892	4964679	-----	2	2	0	-----	0	0	-----	
026	0457914	4964613	-----	2	0	0	-----	0	0	-----	
027	0458034	4964596	-----	2	0	0	-----	0	0	-----	
028	0458190	4964504	-----	2	0	0	-----	0	0	-----	
029	0458313	4964428	BLANK	1	0	0	-----	0	0	-----	
030	0458313	4964428	-----	2	0	0	-----	0	0	-----	
031	0458450	4964392	-----	2	0	0	-----	0	0	-----	
032	0458667	4964407	-----	2	1	0	-----	0	0	-----	loon
033	0458835	4964432	-----	2	1	0	-----	0	0	-----	
034	0459112	4964395	-----	2	0	0	-----	0	0	-----	
035	0459264	4964498	-----	2	0	0	-----	0	0	-----	
036	0459362	4964490	-----	2	0	0	-----	0	0	-----	
037	0459411	4964563	-----	1	0	0	-----	0	0	-----	
038	0459434	4964623	-----	2	0	0	-----	0	0	-----	
039	0459477	4964725	-----	2	0	0	-----	0	0	-----	
040	0459509	4964765	-----	2	0	0	-----	0	0	-----	
041	0459431	4964768	-----	2	0	0	-----	0	0	-----	
042	0459346	4964761	-----	2	0	0	-----	0	0	-----	
043	0459217	4964766	-----	2	1	0	-----	0	0	-----	
044	0459094	4964755	-----	2	0	0	-----	0	0	-----	
045	0458917	4964752	-----	2	0	0	-----	0	0	-----	
046	0458797	4964748	-----	2	0	0	------	0	0	------	
047	0458678	4964724	-----	2	0	0	-----	0	0	-----	
048	0458570	4964717	BLANK	1	0	0	-----	0	0	-----	
049	0458570	4964717	-----	2	0	0	-----	0	0	-----	
050	0458482	4964688	-----	2	0	0	-----	0	0	-----	
051	0458394	4964694	-----	2	0	0	-----	0	0	-----	
052	0458276	4964690	-----	2	0	0	-----	0	0	-----	
053	0458179	4964675	-----	2	0	0	-----	0	0	-----	
054	-------	-------	Filter +	1	8	-----	-----	-----	-----	-----	

Date collected: October 16, 2012 Location: Mississippi River below Lock and Dam 19					Silver Carp			Bighead Carp			
ID	Easting	Northing	Blank	No. of Filters	Presumptive PCR-Positives	Determinative PCR-Positives	Confirmed	Presumptive PCR-Positives	Determinative PCR-Positives	Confirmed	NOTES
001	0638068	4472597	-----	4	8	8	YES	0	0	-----	
002	0638166	4472670	-----	4	7	7	YES	0	0	-----	
003	0638238	4472724	-----	4	8	6	YES	0	0	-----	
004	0638262	4472847	-----	4	1	0	-----	0	0	-----	
005	0638246	4472849	-----	4	2	4	YES	0	0	-----	
006	0638228	4472776	-----	4	8	8	YES	0	0	-----	
007	0638456	4472586	-----	4	8	7	YES	0	0	-----	
008	0638497	4472605	-----	4	7	7	YES	0	0	-----	
009	0638550	4472584	-----	4	7	6	YES	0	0	-----	
010	0638614	4472479	-----	4	7	5	YES	0	0	-----	
011	0638694	4472412	-----	3	0	0	-----	0	0	-----	
012	0638253	4472149	-----	4	1	0	YES	0	0	-----	
013	0638162	4472180	BLANK	4	0	0	-----	0	0	-----	
014	0638162	4472180	-----	4	0	0	-----	0	0	-----	
015	0638004	4472230	-----	4	8	4	YES	0	0	-----	
016	0637815	4472262	-----	4	8	8	YES	0	0	-----	
017	0637775	4472195	-----	4	8	8	YES	0	0	-----	
018	0637524	4472063	-----	4	0	0	-----	0	0	-----	
019	0637457	4472007	-----	4	3	5	YES	0	0	-----	
020	0637235	4471905	-----	4	4	7	YES	0	0	-----	
021	0637223	4471879	-----	4	0	0	-----	0	0	-----	
022	0637118	4471687	-----	4	4	4	YES	0	0	-----	
023	0637091	4471562	-----	4	3	2	YES	0	0	-----	
024	0637191	4471514	-----	4	0	0	-----	0	0	-----	
025	0637257	4471443	-----	4	6	-----	-----	0	0	-----	
026	0637270	4471388	-----	4	4	-----	-----	0	0	-----	
027	0637244	4471312	-----	4	4	-----	-----	0	0	-----	
028	0637243	4471189	-----	4	0	0	-----	0	0	-----	
029	0637343	4471235	BLANK	1	0	0	-----	0	0	-----	
030	0637343	4471235	-----	4	0	0	-----	0	0	-----	
031	0637195	4471122	-----	4	4	-----	-----	0	0	-----	
032	0637298	4471124	-----	4	0	0	-----	0	0	-----	
033	0637070	4471109	-----	4	8	-----	-----	0	0	-----	
034	0636931	4471140	-----	2	8	-----	-----	0	0	-----	
035	0636924	4471093	-----	4	1	-----	-----	0	0	-----	
036	0636705	4470983	-----	4	0	0	-----	0	0	-----	
037	0636574	4470980	-----	4	0	0	-----	0	0	-----	
038	0636463	4471032	-----	4	4	-----	-----	0	0	-----	
039	0636405	4471069	-----	4	0	0	-----	0	0	-----	
040	0636338	4471112	-----	4	0	0	-----	0	0	-----	
041	0636268	4471191	-----	4	0	0	-----	0	0	-----	
042	0636186	4471315	-----	4	8	-----	-----	0	0	-----	
043	0635730	4471479	-----	4	8	-----	-----	0	0	-----	
044	0635465	4471551	-----	4	8	-----	-----	0	0	-----	
045	0635529	4471588	-----	4	7	-----	-----	0	0	-----	
046	0635633	4471597	-----	4	8	-----	-----	0	0	-----	
047	0635709	4471601	-----	4	8	-----	-----	0	0	-----	
048	0635905	4471591	BLANK	1	0	0	-----	0	0	-----	
049	0635905	4471591	-----	4	0	0	-----	0	0	-----	
050	0636239	4471614	-----	4	8	-----	-----	0	0	-----	
051	0636380	4471568	-----	4	0	0	-----	0	0	-----	
052	0637025	4471838	-----	4	0	0	-----	0	0	-----	
053	0636533	4471724	-----	4	7	-----	-----	0	0	-----	
054	Not collected										

Appendix 2.   Representative electrophoresis gels for the detection of the DNA of silver carp in samples taken from each site. Gels used for the detection of bighead carp were not included because bighead carp DNA was not detected. Representative gels for presumptive and determinative PCR-positives are included.

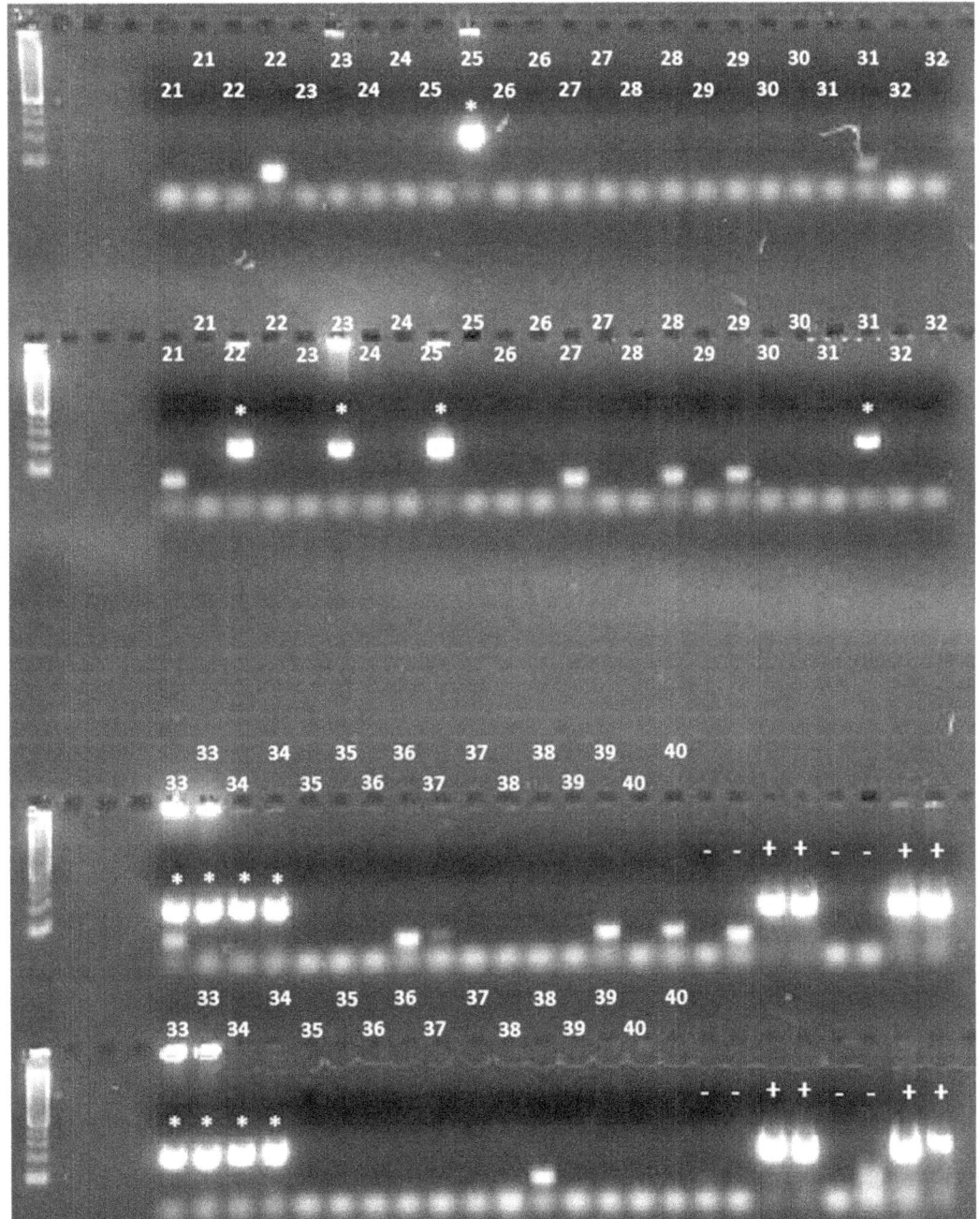

Appendix 2A.   Representative electrophoresis gels demonstrating the detection of the DNA of silver carp in samples taken from the Mississippi River below Lock and Dam 19. Lanes considered presumptive PCR-positive are marked with "*"; the positive extraction and positive PCR control lanes are marked with a white "+".

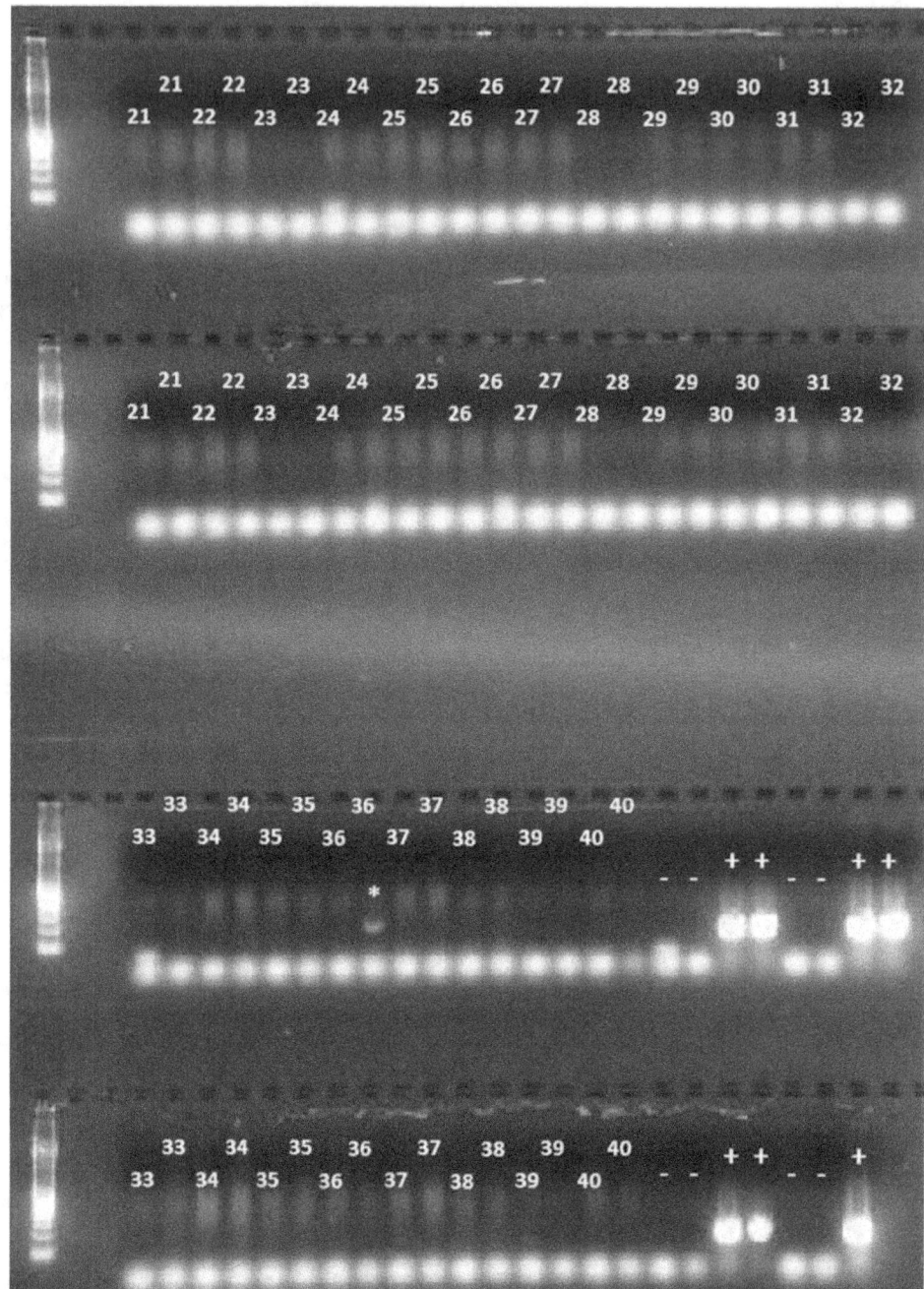

Appendix 2B.   Representative electrophoresis gels demonstrating the detection of the DNA of silver carp in samples taken from Square Lake. Lanes considered presumptive PCR-positive are marked with "*"; the positive extraction and positive PCR control lanes are marked with a white "+".

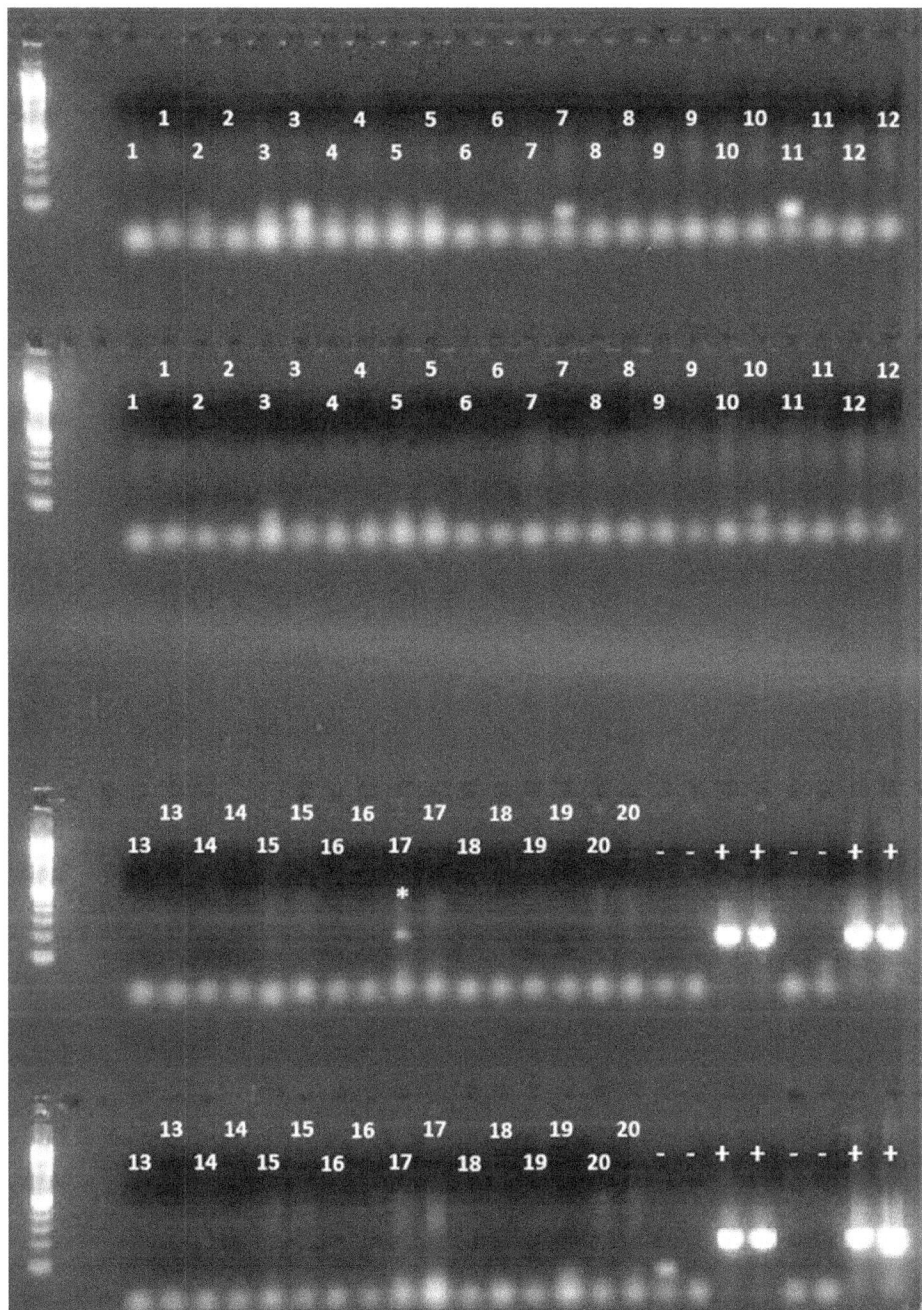

Appendix 2C.   Representative electrophoresis gels demonstrating the detection of the DNA of silver carp in samples taken from Lake Riley. Lanes considered presumptive PCR-positive are marked with "*"; the positive extraction and positive PCR control lanes are marked with a white "+".

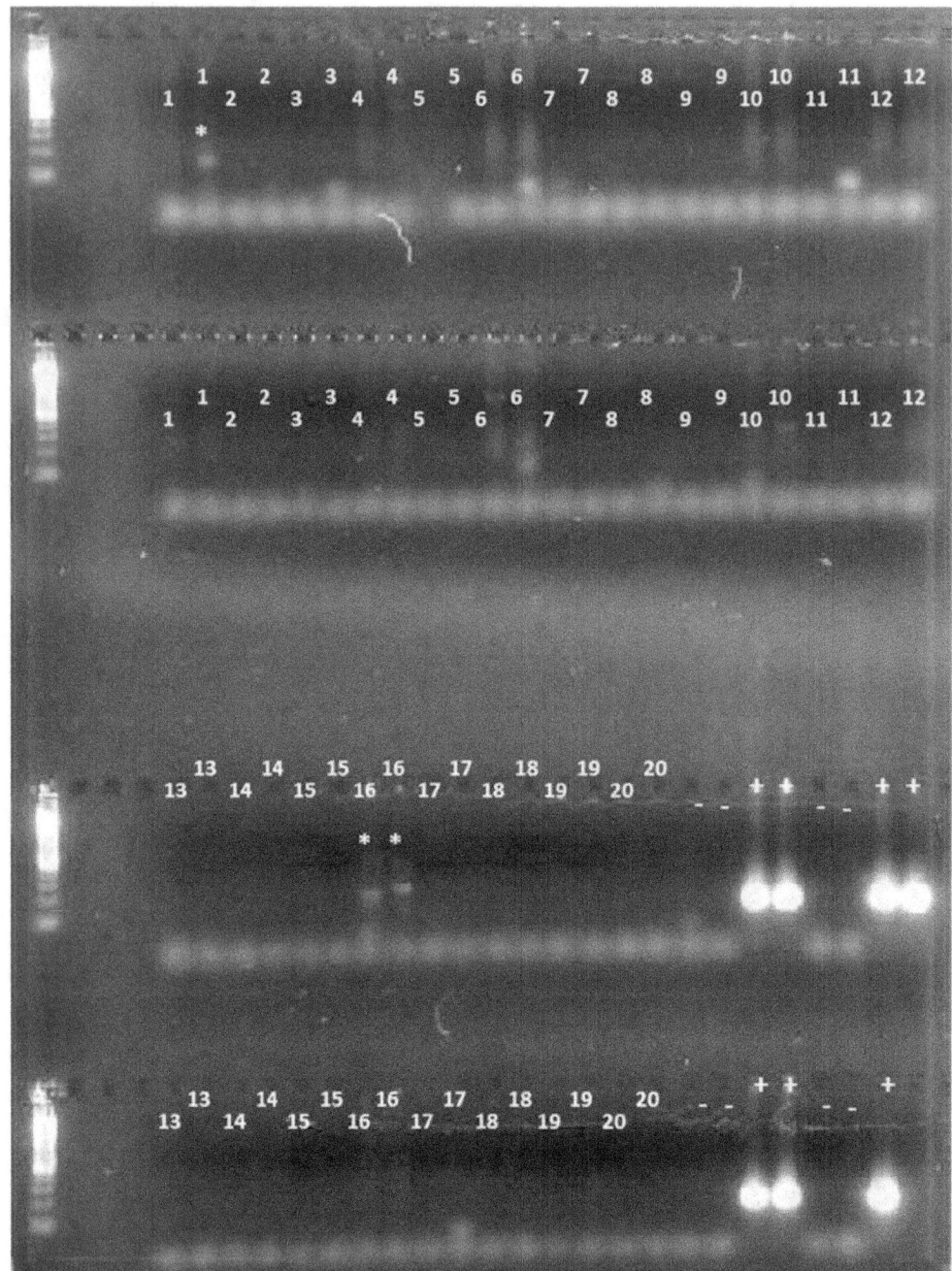

Appendix 2D.   Representative electrophoresis gels demonstrating the detection of the DNA of silver carp in samples taken from the Mississippi River above the Coon Rapids Dam. Lanes considered presumptive PCR-positive are marked with "*"; the positive extraction and positive PCR control lanes are marked with a white "+".

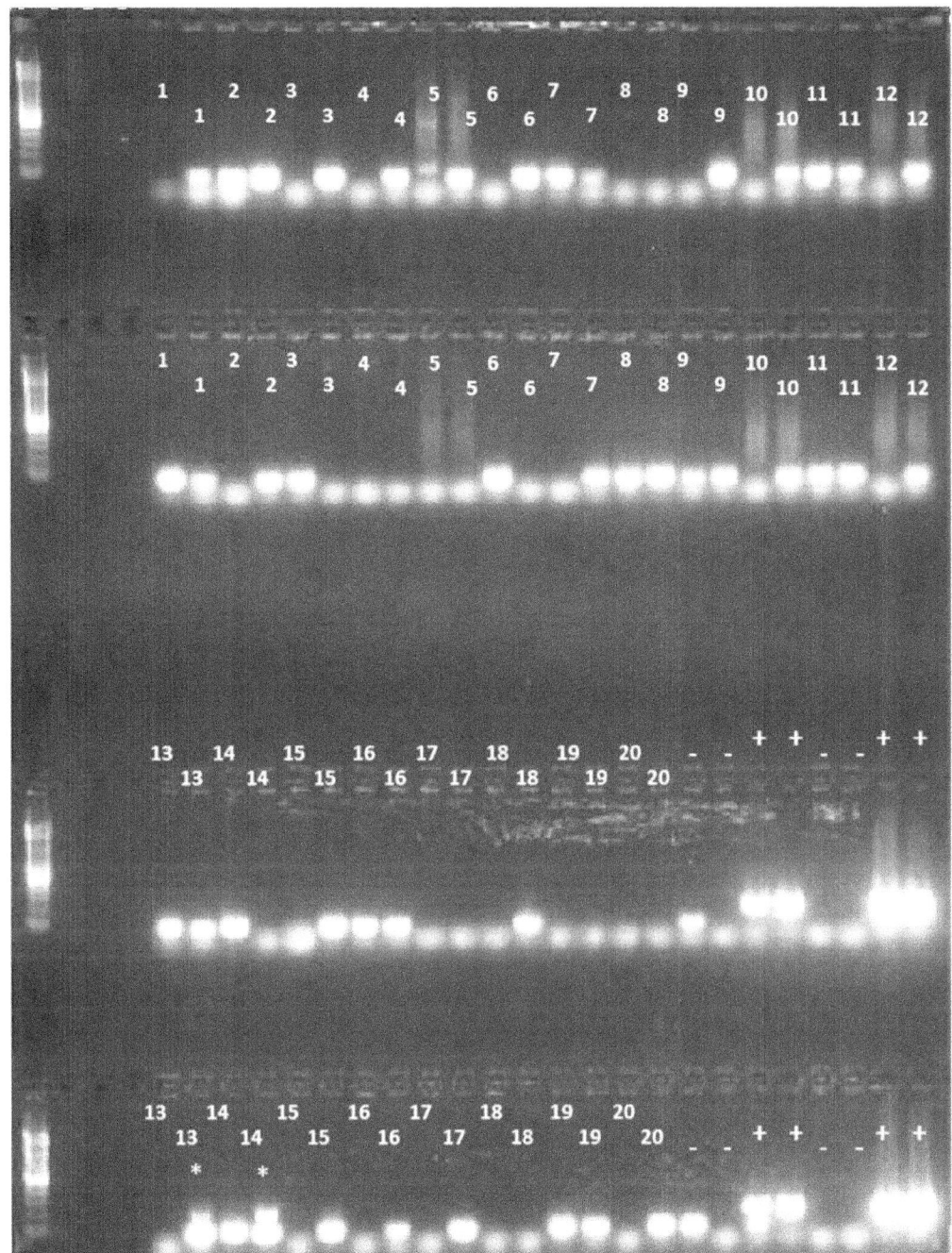

Appendix 2E. Representative electrophoresis gels demonstrating the detection of the DNA of silver carp in samples taken from the Mississippi River below the Coon Rapids Dam. Lanes considered presumptive PCR-positive are marked with "*"; the positive extraction and positive PCR control lanes are marked with a white "+".

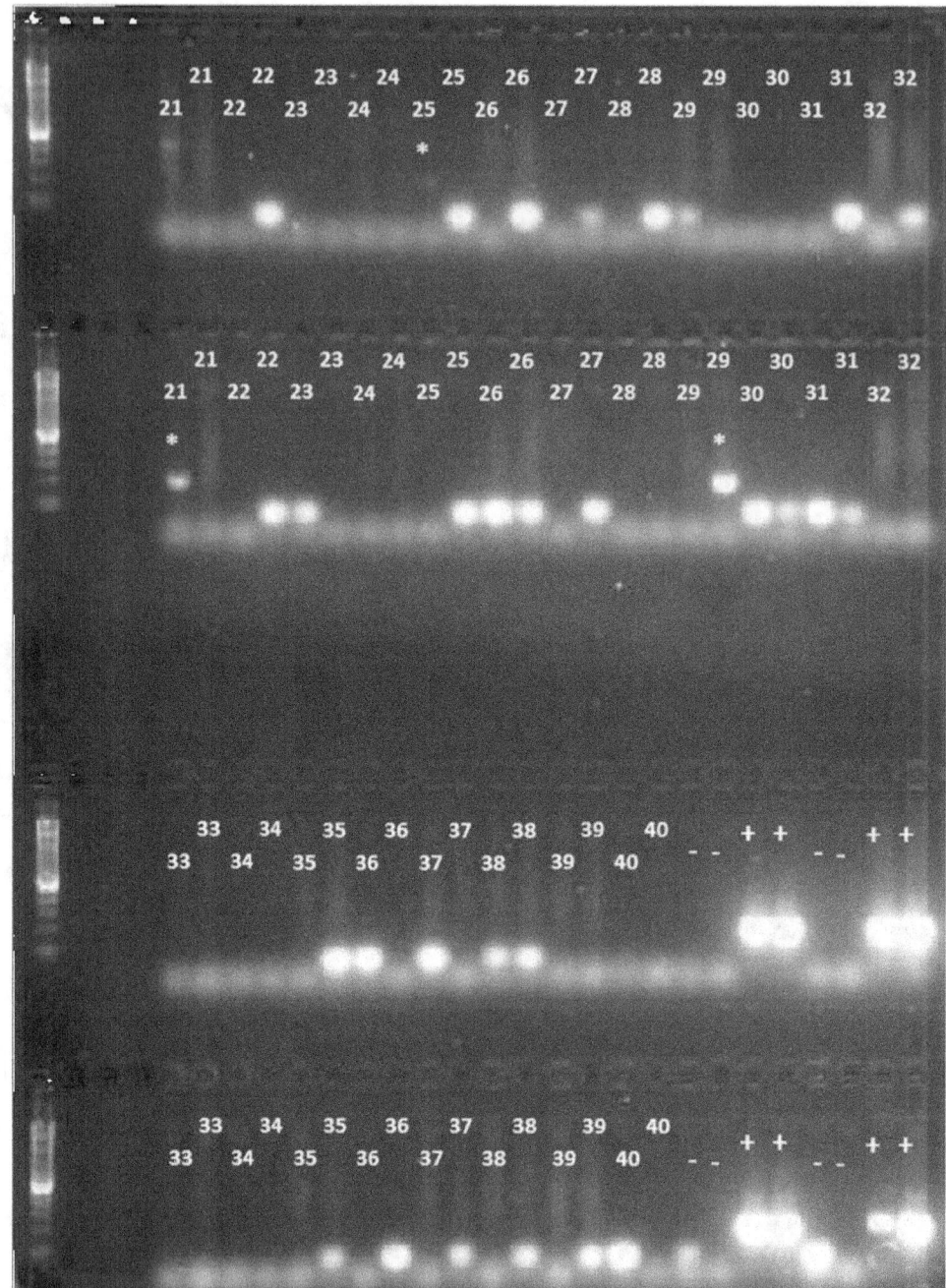

Appendix 2F.   Representative electrophoresis gels demonstrating the detection of the DNA of silver carp in samples taken from the Mississippi River below Lock and Dam 1. Lanes considered presumptive PCR-positive are marked with "*"; the positive extraction and positive PCR control lanes are marked with a white "+".

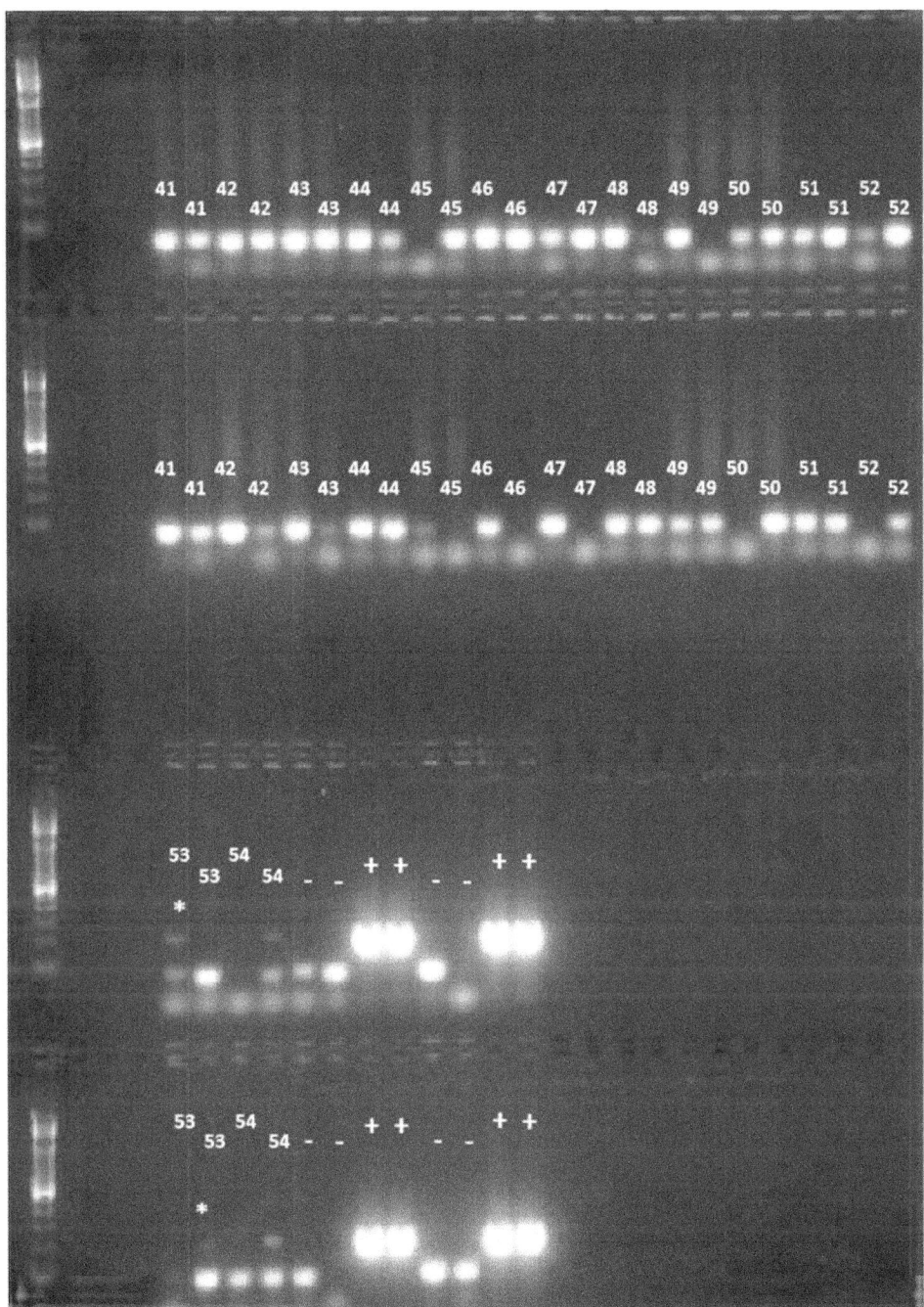

Appendix 2G.   Representative electrophoresis gels demonstrating the detection of the DNA of silver carp in samples taken from the St. Croix River above the St. Croix Falls Dam. Lanes considered presumptive PCR-positive are marked with "*"; the positive extraction and positive PCR control lanes are marked with a white "+".

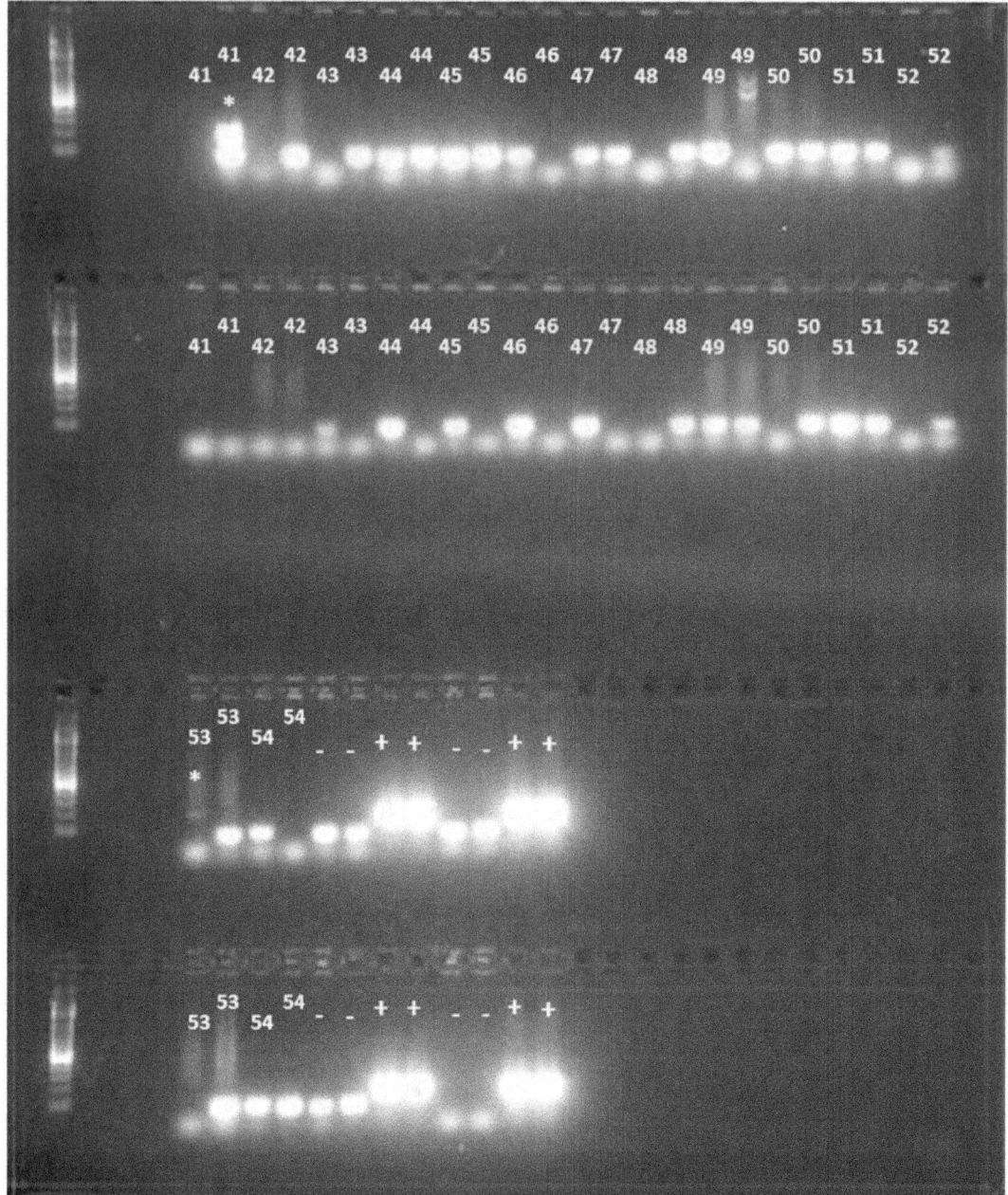

Appendix 2*H***.**   Representative electrophoresis gels demonstrating the detection of the DNA of silver carp in samples taken from the St. Croix River below the St. Croix Falls Dam. Lanes considered presumptive PCR-positive are marked with "*"; the positive extraction and positive PCR control lanes are marked with a white "+".

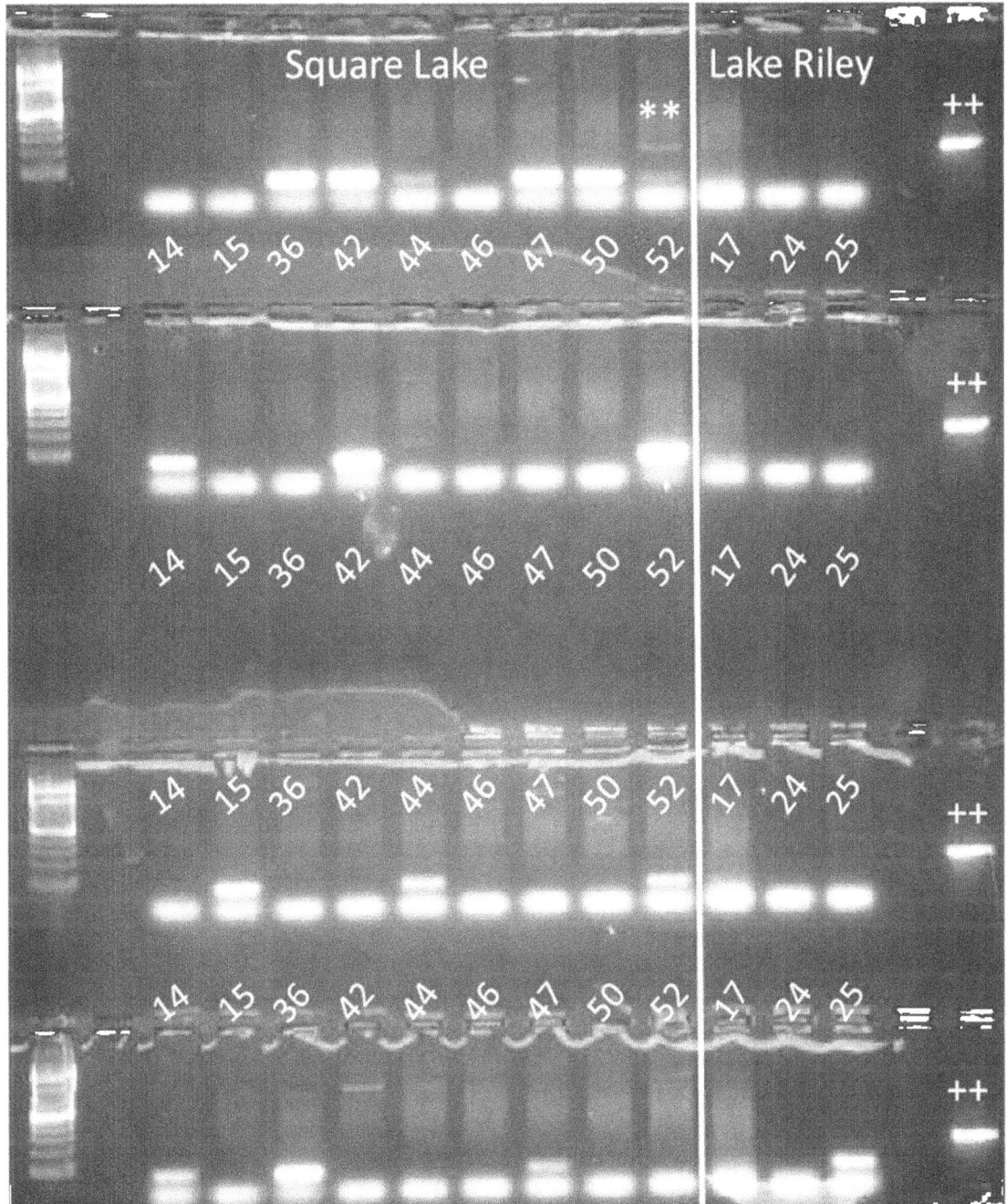

Appendix 2*I*.   Representative electrophoresis gels of samples considered to be presumptive PCR positive from Square Lake and Lake Riley. Lanes considered determinative PCR-positives are marked with "**"; the positive PCR control lanes are marked "++".

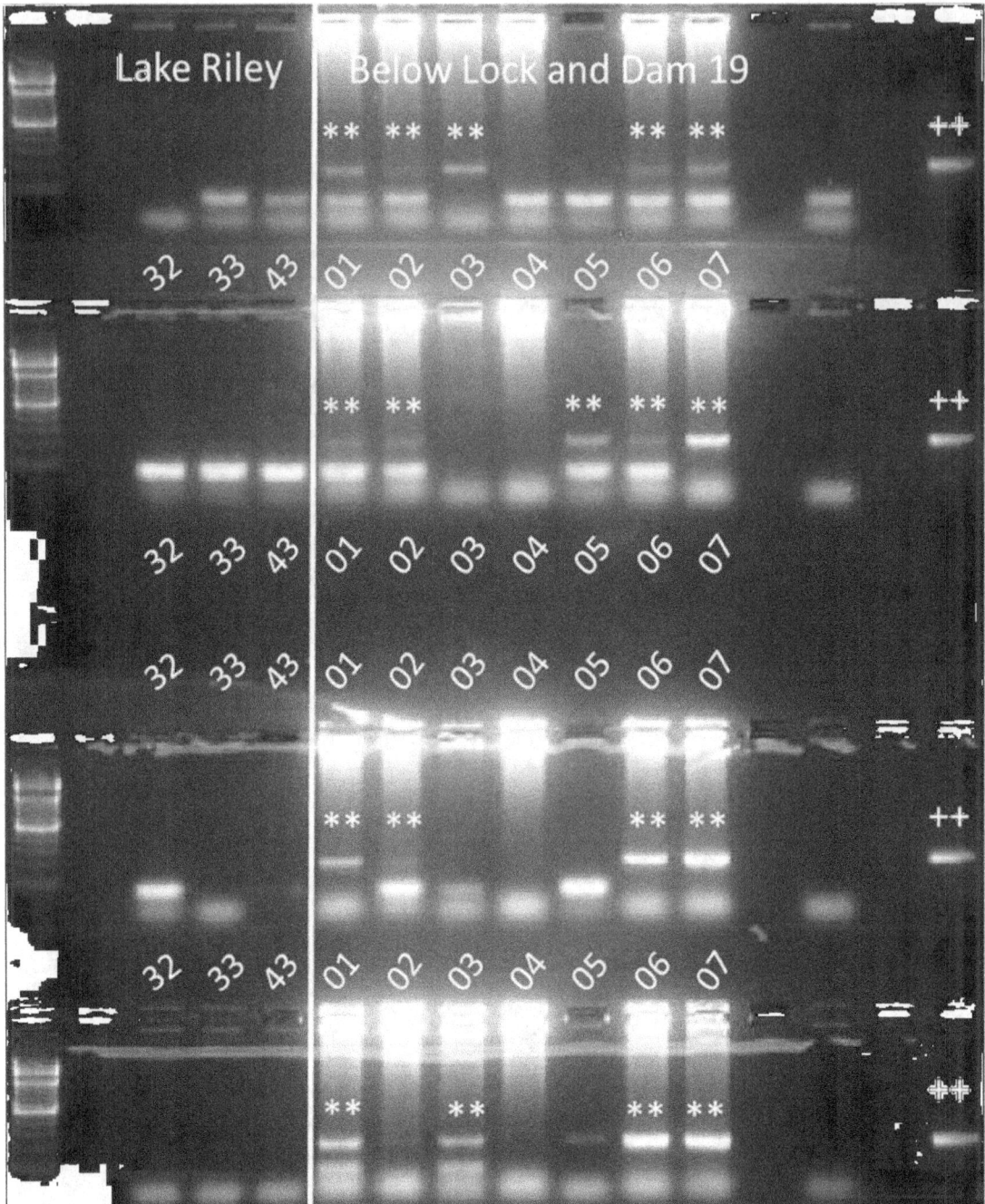

Appendix 2J.   Representative electrophoresis gels for samples considered to be presumptive PCR positive from Lake Riley and from the Mississippi River below Lock and Dam 19. Lanes considered determinative PCR-positive are marked with "**"; the positive PCR control lanes are marked "++".

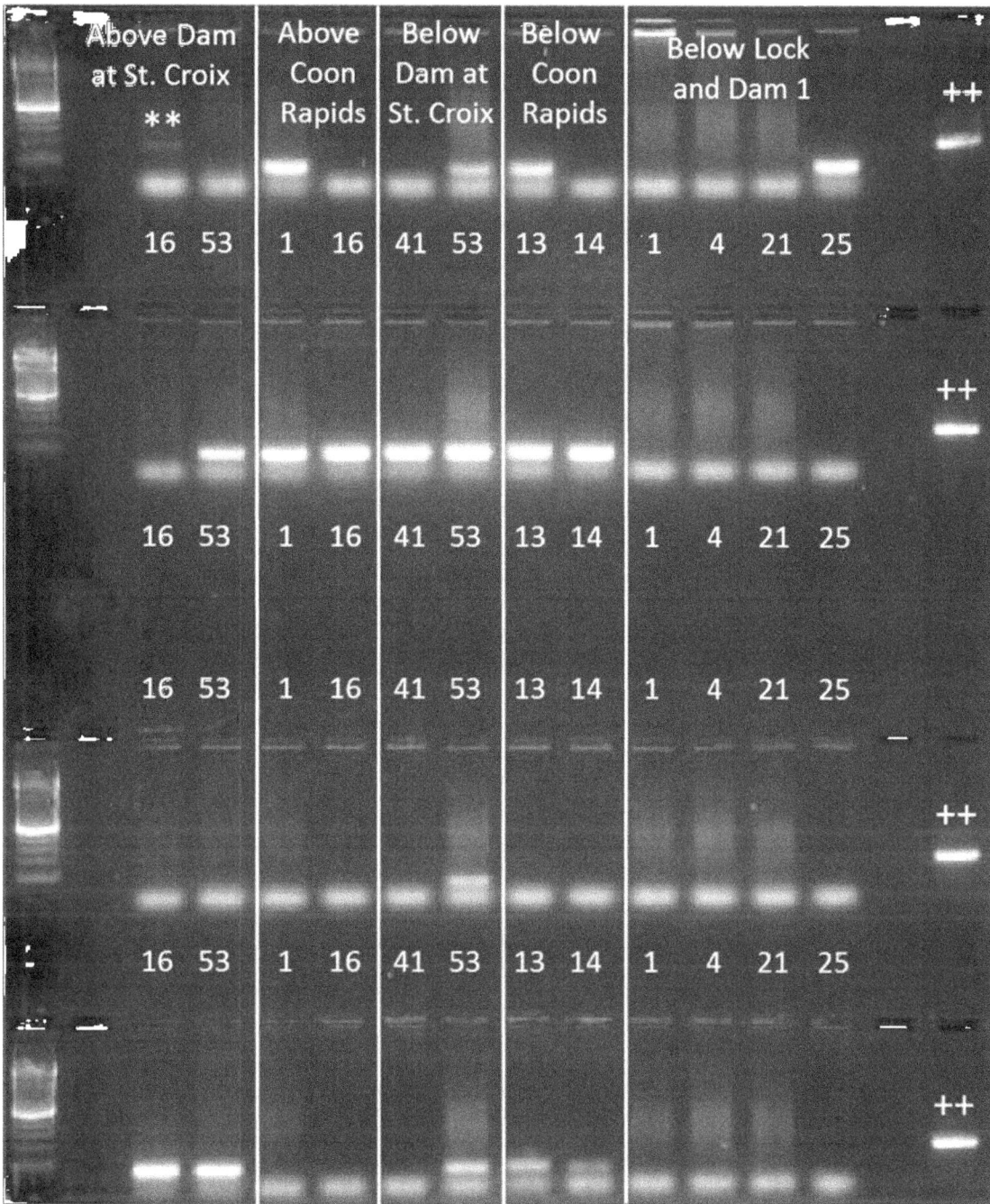

Appendix 2K.   Representative electrophoresis gels for samples considered presumptive PCR positive from above the St. Croix Falls Dam, above the Coon Rapids Dam, below the St. Croix Falls Dam, below the Coon Rapids Dam and below Lock and Dam 1. Lanes considered determinative PCR-positive are marked with "**"; the positive PCR control lanes are marked "++".

Appendix 3. Sequences of determinative PCR-positive environmental samples amplified with the silver carp marker. The percent match of each sequence to published silver carp DNA sequences in GenBank (*http://www.ncbi.nlm.nih. gov/genbank/*) is included following the sequence. A sample was determined "confirmed positive" only when both the forward and reverse sequences of that sample were greater than 95% similar to published silver carp sequences.

Lock and Dam 19 - 2012 1016 001 – CONFIRMED POSITIVE

Forward

TGGGGGTCTCAATTTTTCTTGAATATTAACTTCTATTTAACTTAACTATATTAATGTAGTAAGAAAC-
CACCTACTGGTTTATATTAAGGTATTCTATTCATGATAAGATCAGGGACAATAATCGTGGGGGTGGCGCA-
CAATGAACTATTACTTGCATTTGGCTTAACTTAAATCCAATGGTTGATCCAATGGCACGGCCTCCCAAAA-
CAGAAGGGTTAAACCAAAAAACCTGAACTTATCCCTTCCTAATCCTATTAAAATTAAAAAAAC-
CACCCCCCTAAAAGAAAAAATTACTTTATTTTAAACATCTTTTTGTAAACCCTCCCACCGCGCTTTGTA-
AATTTCAATAACATATTCTTTTTTTTTATATTTACAGCACATCCGTGCGACGTCAAAGAAATGAAACCA-
CACTACAGATGAAATGATAGAAAACTTTAGA

96% match to silver carp on >150 nucleotide portion of sequence

Reverse

GGGGACCCCACGATTATTGTCCCTGATCTTATCATGAATAGAATACCTTAATATAAACCAGTAGGTG-
GTTTCTTACTACATTAATATAGTTAAGTTAAATAGAAGTTAATATTTCAAGGAAATATTTGAGGACCAAT-
TATAGTGGAACACCTCTTTTCTCAGGATTTTCTTTATTTTTATGGTTAAGGGAGGGGCCCCCGCCCCA-
CAAAACGGGAAGGGAACACCCCCGGTCCTGGCCCCATACCTCCTCAACCACTCAAAATTACGT-
GCACCCCCCCCGAAAAAAGAACTTTTTCTTTTTTTTTTTTTTTTTTTTTACCAGCCCCCCGCCTTTTT-
GTTTTTTTAAATTCCTTTTCTCTTTTTTTTTTTTTCTCAGAACCGCGGAGACGCGTGAAGCCAATGAACAC-
TACCTACAGAGAAGATGATAGGTTACTC

98% match to silver carp on >150 nucleotide portion of sequence

Lock and Dam 19 - 2012 1016 002– CONFIRMED POSITIVE

Forward

GGGGCTCTAAACATCTTCCTTTGCAATATTAACTTCTATTTAACTTAACTATATTAATTGTAGTAAGAAAC-
CACCTACTGGTTTATATTAAGGTATTCTATTCATGATAAGATCAGGGACAATAATCGTGGGGGTGGCG-
CAGAATGAACTATTACTTGCATTTGGCACACACCCCCGGGCCCTGCTGGGGAGAAACAAAAAAAAAA-
CACAACACCCCACCCACAGTACGGACCGGCCTTTTATAAGGGTCTTAT

95% match to silver carp on >150 nucleotide portion of sequence

Reverse

GGGGCCCCGCACGCATTATTTGTCCCTGATCTTATCATGAATAGAATACCTTAATATAAACCAGTAGGTG-
GTTTCTTACTACATTAATATAGTTAAGTTAAATAGAAGTTAATATTTCAAGGAAATATTTGACAACCAAT-
TATAGTGGAACACCTCTTTTCTCAGGACCCCCGTTCCCCCCCAGCTATATCCACAAAATCCACCGC-
CACTCCAGCCCGGTGCTTCCCCCCTTCCCATCTAGGTCTATT

96% match to silver carp on >150 nucleotide portion of sequence

Lock and Dam 19 - 2012 1016 003– CONFIRMED POSITIVE

Forward

TGTTGGTTCTCAAATATTTCCTTGAATATTAACTTCTATTTAACTTAACTATATTAATGTAGTAAGAAAC-
CACCTACTGGTTTATATTAAGGTATTCTATTCATGATAAGATCAGGGACAATAATCGTGGGGGGTG-
GCGCAGAATGAACTATTACTTGCATTTGGCATTTTTCTTTTTTCTTTTGGTTTATGCAAGGGCCTG-
GTCCCCCAAAACGGGAAGGGTAAATCCCCGGACCTGACCCTATCCCTTCATCAACCACTCCTAATTA-
CAATCTCCACCCCAAAAACAAAACTTTTCCTTTTTTTAAATTTTTCTTTTTAAGTGGTCCTTCGCTTTT-
GATTTTTTAATACCGTTTCTCTCCTTTTCATTTCAGCGTTACCGGCGTGCTTTGTGAAAGAC

99% match to silver carp on >150 nucleotide portion of sequence

Reverse

TGGACCCCACGATTATTGTCCCTGATCTTATCATGAATAGAATACCTTAATATAAACCAGTAGGTG-
GTTTCTTACTACATTAATATAGTTAAGTTAAATAGAAGTTAATATTTCAAGGAAATATTTGAGAAC-
CAATTATAGTGGAACACCTCTTTTCTCAGGGTTTTTCTTTTTTTTTTTGTTTTATGGAATGGCCC-
GCCCAAAAAAAACGGAAAGGGAAAAATACCCATTCTGGTCCCTTACTTTCACTCCACTTATAATTAACT-
GTATCGCCACGAAAAAAAAATTTTTTTTTTTTTTTTTTTTTTTTTTGTAAACCCCCCGGGGGGCGTTTTGT-
TATTTAATATAATATTTCTCCCTTTTATATTTATCAAACCCGGTGTGAGATGTGA

98% match to silver carp on >150 nucleotide portion of sequence

Lock and Dam 19 - 2012 1016 005 – CONFIRMED POSITIVE

Forward

GTTGGGTTCAATATTTCCTTGAATATTAACTTCTATTTAACTTAACTATATTAATGTAGTAAGAAAC-
CACCTACTGGTTTATATTAAGGTATTCTATTCATGATAAGATCAGGGACAATAATCGTGGGGGGTG-
GCGCAGAATGAACTATTACTTGCATTTGGCACACCCCCCGTGCCTGGCTGGGAGAAC-
CAAAAAAAAAAAACCCAACCCCCACCCCCGGGGGGGGGCCCCCTTATAAACAAGGGTTATA

99% match to silver carp on >150 nucleotide portion of sequence

Reverse

CCCCCACGGATTATTGTCCTGATCTTATCATGAATAGAATACCTTAATATAAACCAGTAGGTGGTTTCT-
TACTACATTAATATAGTTAAGTTAAATAGAAGTTAATATTTCAAGGAAATATTTGAGAACCAATTATAGTG-
GAACACCTCTTTTCTCAGGGCCCCCGTCCCTCCTGGGAGAGACAAGAAAAAAACGGACACCCCATC-
CGGGTAGGGACCTGCCATTAGTCGGGT

98% match to silver carp on >150 nucleotide portion of sequence

Lock and Dam 19 - 2012 1016 006 – CONFIRMED POSITIVE

Forward

TGGGGTTCATTTTCTTGAATATTAACTTCTATTTAACTTAACTATATTAATGTAGTAAGAAACCACCTACTG-
GTTTATATTAAGGTATTCTATTCATGATAAGATCAGGGACAATAATCGTGGGGGTGGCGCAGAATGAAC-
TATTACTTGCATTTGGCAACCCGGGTCCCGCATGGGGGGGACAACAAAAAACTGGACACCCCCAACC-
GGGGGGGGGCCCCCCTTCCCTGCTGAGAAA

99% match to silver carp on >150 nucleotide portion of sequence

Reverse

GGACCCACGATTATTGTCCTGATCTTATCATGAATAGAATACCTTAATATAAACCAGTAGGTGGTTTCT-
TACTACATTAATATAGTTAAGTTAAATAGAAGTTAATATTTCAAGGAAATATTTGAGAACCAATTATAGTG-
GAACACCTCTTTTCTCAGG

98% match to silver carp on >150 nucleotide portion of sequence

Lock and Dam 19 - 2012 1016 007 – CONFIRMED POSITIVE

Forward

TGGGGTCTAATATTTCTTGAATATTAACTTCTATTTAACTTAACTATATTAATGTAGTAAGAAAC-
CACCTACTGGTTTATATTAAGGTATTCTATTCATGATAAGATCAGGGACAATAATCGTGGGGGTGGCG-
CAGAATGAACTATTACTTGCATTTGGCA

98% match to silver carp on >150 nucleotide portion of sequence

Reverse

CCCCCACGATTATTGTCCTGATCTTATCATGAATAGAATACCTTAATATAAACCAGTAGGTGGTTTCTTACTACAT-
TAATATAGTTAAGTTAAATAGAAGTTAATATTTCAAGGAAATATTTGAGAACCAATTATAGTGGAACACCTCTT-
TTCTCAGG

98% match to silver carp on >150 nucleotide portion of sequence

Lock and Dam 19 - 2012 1016 008 – CONFIRMED POSITIVE

Forward

GGGGGTCCATTTTCCTTGAATATTAACTTCTATTTAACTTAACTATATTAATGTAGTAAGAAAC-
CACCTACTGGTTTATATTAAGGTATTCTATTCATGATAAGATCAGGGACAATAATCGTGGGGGTGGCG-
CAGAATGAACTATTACTTGCATTTGGCA

99% match to silver carp on >150 nucleotide portion of sequence

Reverse

CCCCCCGATTATTGTCCTGATCTTATCATGAATAGAATACCTTAATATAAACCAGTAGGTGGTTTCTTAC-
TACATTAATATAGTTAAGTTAAATAGAAGTTAATATTTCAAGGAAATATTTGAGAACCAATTATAGTGGAA-
CACCTCTTTTCTCAGG

97% match to silver carp on >150 nucleotide portion of sequence

Lock and Dam 19 - 2012 1016 009 – CONFIRMED POSITIVE

Forward

GGGGGTCTCAATTTTCCTTGAATATTAACTTCTATTTAACTTAACTATATTAATGTAGTAAGAAAC-
CACCTACTGGTTTATATTAAGGTATTCTATTCATGATAAGATCAGGGACAATAATCGTGGGGGTGGCG-
CAGAATGAACTATTACTTGCATTTGGCA

97% match to silver carp on >150 nucleotide portion of sequence

Reverse

GGGACCCACGATTATTGTCCTGATCTTATCATGAATAGAATACCTTAATATAAACAAGTAGGTGGTTTCT-
TACTACATTAATATAGTTAAGTTAAATAGAAGTTAATATTTCAAGGAAATATTTGAGAACCAATTATAGTG-
GAACACCTCTTTTCTCAGG

97% match to silver carp on >150 nucleotide portion of sequence

Lock and Dam 19 - 2012 1016 010 – CONFIRMED POSITIVE

Forward

GTGGGGTCCAATTTTTCCTTGAATATTAACTTCTATTTAACTTAACTATATTAATGTAGTAAGAAAC-
CACCTACTGGTTTATATTAAGGTATTCTATTCATGATAAGATCAGGGACAATAATCGTGGGGGTGGCG-
CAGAATGAACTATTACTTGCCTTTGGCA

97% match to silver carp on >150 nucleotide portion of sequence

Reverse

GGCCCCCACGATTATTGTCCTGATCTTATCATGAATAGAATACCTTAATATAAACAAGTAGGTGGTTTCT-
TACTACATTAATATAGTTAAGTTAAATAGAAGTTAATATTTCAAGGAAATATTTGAGGACCAATTATAGTG-
GAACACCTCTTTTCTCAGGCC

97% match to silver carp on >150 nucleotide portion of sequence

Lock and Dam 19 - 2012 1016 015 – CONFIRMED POSITIVE

Forward

GGGGGTCCTCATATTTCTTGAATATTAACTTCTATTTAACTTAACTATATTAATGTAGTAAGAAAC-
CACCTACTGGTTTATATTAAGGTATTCTATTCATGATAAGATCAGGGACAATAATCGTGGGGGTG-
GCCCATAATGAACTATTACTTGCATTTGGCACCC

96% match to silver carp on >150 nucleotide portion of sequence

Reverse

GGGACCCACGATTATTGTCCTGATCTTATCATGAATAGAATACCTTAATATAAACAAGTAGGTGGTTTCT-
TACTACATTAATATAGTTAAGTTAAATAGAAGTTAATATTTCAAGGAAATATTTGAG

98% match to silver carp on >150 nucleotide portion of sequence

Lock and Dam 19 - 2012 1016 016 – CONFIRMED POSITIVE

Forward

GCTGGTCTCATATTTCTTGAATATTAACTTCTATTTAACTTAACTATATTAATGTAGTAAGAAAC-
CACCTACTGGTTTATATTAAGGTATTCTATTCATGATAAGATCAGGGACAATAATCGTGGGGGTGGCG-
CAGAATGAACTATTACTTGCATTTGGCA

99% match to silver carp on >150 nucleotide portion of sequence

Reverse

GCCCCACGATTATTGTCCTGATCTTATCATGAATAGAATACCTTAATATAAACCAGTAGGTGGTTTCTTAC-
TACATTAATATAGTTAAGTTAAATAGAAGTTAATATTTCAAGGAAATATTTGAGAACCAATTATAGTGGAA-
CACCTCTTTTCTCAGGA

98% match to silver carp on >150 nucleotide portion of sequence

Lock and Dam 19 - 2012 1016 017 – CONFIRMED POSITIVE

Forward

GTTGGGTCTCATTTTCCTTGAATATTAACTTCTATTTAACTTAACTATATTAATGTAGTAAGAAAC-
CACCTACTGGTTTATATTAAGGTATTCTATTCATGATAAGATCAGGGACAATAATCGTGGGG

95% match to silver carp on >150 nucleotide portion of sequence

Reverse

GGGCCGCACGATTATTGTCCTGATCTTATCATGAATAGAATACCTTAATATAAACAAGTAGGTGGTTTCT-
TACTACATTAATATAGTTAAGTTAAATAGAAGTTAATATTTCAAGGAAATATTTGAGAACCAATTATAGTG-
GAACACCTCTTTTCTCAGG

97% match to silver carp on >150 nucleotide portion of sequence

Lock and Dam 19 - 2012 1016 019 – CONFIRMED POSITIVE

Forward

GCGGGGTCCAAAATTTCTTGAATATTAACTTCTATTTAACTTAACTATATTAATGTAGTAAGAAAC-
CACCTACTGGTTTATATTAAGGTATTCTATTCATGATAAGATCAGGGACAATAATCGTGGGGGTGGCG-
CAGAATGAACTATTACTTGCATTTGGCACCCCCGGGCCCCCCGGCTATAACACCAAAATCCACGGC-
CACCCCCGGCCCGGTGCTTCCCCCCTTCCCTTCTGAAGATTAACC

97% match to silver carp on >150 nucleotide portion of sequence

Reverse

GGGGCCCCACGATTATTGTCCTGATCTTATCATGAATAGAATACCTTAATATAAACCAGTAGGTGGTTTCT-
TACTACATTAATATAGTTAAGTTAAATAGAAGTTAATATTTCAAGGAAATATTTGAGAACCAATTATAGTG-
GAACACCTCTTTTCTCAGGG

98% match to silver carp on >150 nucleotide portion of sequence

Lock and Dam 19 - 2012 1016 020 – CONFIRMED POSITIVE

Forward

GTTTGGTCTCATATTTCCTTGAATATTAACTTCTATTTAACTTAACTATATAAATGTAGTAAGAAAC-
CACCTACTGGTTTATATTAAGGTATTCTATTCATGATAAGATCAGGGACAATAATCGTGGGGGTGGCG-
CAGAATGAACTATTACTTGCATTTGGCAACAACATACGAGCCGGAAGCATAAAGTGTAAAGCCTGGGCT-
GCCTAATGACTGAGCTAACTCATATTAATTGTTTTCTGTTTATTGTCTGCTTTTCCCCCGGAAACTT-
GTCTTGTCACCTGCATTAATGAATCGGCCAACCTGCGGGGACACGCGG

99% match to silver carp on >150 nucleotide portion of sequence

Reverse

GGGTCCCACGATTATTGTCCTGATCTTATCATGAATAGAATACCTTAATATAAACAAGTAGGTGGTTTCT-
TACTACATTAATATAGTTAAGTTAAATAGAAGTTAATATTTCAAGGAAATATTTGAGA

98% match to silver carp on >150 nucleotide portion of sequence

Lock and Dam 19 - 2012 1016 022 – CONFIRMED POSITIVE

Forward

GCGGGTCTAATTTTCCTTGAATATTAACTTCTATTTAACTTAACTATATTAATGTAGTAAGAAAC-
CACCTACTGGTTTATATTAAGGTATTCTATTCATGATAAGATCAGGGACAATAATCGTGGGGGTGGCGC

99% match to silver carp on >150 nucleotide portion of sequence

Reverse

GGGGCCCACGATTATTGTCCTGATCTTATCATGAATAGAATACCTTAATATAAACAAGTAGGTGGTTTCT-
TACTACATTAATATAGTTAAGTTAAATAGAAGTTAATATTTCAAGGAAATATTTGAGAACCAATTATAGTG-
GAACACCTCTTTTTTCAGG

97% match to silver carp on >150 nucleotide portion of sequence

Lock and Dam 19 - 2012 1016 023 – CONFIRMED POSITIVE

Forward

TTTGGTCTAATTTTCCTTGAATATTAACTTCTATTTACTTAACTATATTAATGTAGTAAGAAACCACCTACTG-
GTTTATATTAAGGTATTCTATTCATGATAAGATCAGGGACAATAATCGTGGGGGTGGCGCAGAATGAAC-
TATTACTTGCATTTGGCA

99% match to silver carp on >150 nucleotide portion of sequence

Reverse

GTGACCCACGATTATTGTCCTGATCTTATCATGAATAGAATACCTTAATATAAACAAGTAGGTGGTTTCT-
TACTACATTAATATAGTTAAGTTAAATAGAAGTTAATATTTCAACGAAATATTTGACGACCAATTATAGTG-
GAACACCTCTTTTCTCAGGCAC

97% match to silver carp on >150 nucleotide portion of sequence

Square Lake - 2012 1001 052 – CONFIRMED NEGATIVE

Forward

CGGGGCCCAAAATCCTCCTTGGATTATCAACTTCTATTTAACTTGACTATATTAATGGGTAATAACC-
GGGGACTGGTTTATAGAAAGGTTTCTCCTCATGAGGAGATCCGGGAACGCCGCGTGGGGGTGGCGGT-
TATTGAACTCTTCCTTGGCCTGTCACACCCCGGCCCCGCTGGGGGGGCCAGCGAATAAAC

77% match to silver carp on 135 nucleotide portion of sequence

Reverse

GCCCCCCACGATTATTGTCCTTGATCTTATCTGAATAGAATACCTTAATATAAACCAGTAGGTGGTTTCT-
TACTACATTAATATAGTTAAGTTAAATAGAAGTTAATATTTCAAGGAAATATTTGACAACCAATTATAGTG-
GAACACCTCTTTTCTCTGGATC

96% match to silver carp on >150 nucleotide portion of sequence

St. Croix, above dam - 2012 0917 016 – CONFIRMED NEGATIVE

Forward

CGGCCCCCTTTTTTTCGCTTGTTTTTTCCCTCTGTTTGAGCGTCGGAATCTCTTGAGCCTATTCTCTTA-
CAAAGCATCTTATAGGTCTTCGTTAATTTTCGGCTTGTTTTCAATGACCCATTACTAGGATTTCGCACGTT-
TACTATCCTCCCCCCATGTTTCTGCCCACCCCCGTTT

0% match to silver carp

Reverse

TGGCCCGAACATTTATTGAATGACCCACGAGATGCTTTATTAAGAGAATATGCTCAAGAAATAGC-
GAGGGTCAAACAGATGCTGGAACAACAAGAAATAGGAGAGCCTATTATAGTGGAACACCTCTTTTCT-
CAGGGGTT

87% match to silver carp on only a 44 nucleotide portion of sequence

St. Croix, above dam - 2012 0917 043 – CONFIRMED NEGATIVE

Forward

CGGGGGCCTCACTGGTACCTGGGTTTTTTAACTCCTCTTGACTGACCCTTTTGTGAGA-
AAGAGCCCCTACTCCATATATTAAGGCTCTCTCCATGAGATGATCAGGGACAACAGTCATGGGCGGGC-
GTTTAATGAACTCCCCCTAGCTTTTCCAAACCCCCGGGCCCGGCTGGCAAGTACAAAATTAAAACCC

78% match to silver carp on only a 63 nucleotide portion of sequence

Reverse

TCCCCCCCCCCAAATTATTTTTCCCTATTTTTATCTGAATAAATTACCTTAATATA-
ACCCATTAGGGGGTTTCTTACTATTTTAATATACGTAACTTAAATAGAATTTATTATTTCAGGGAAATTTT-
GATTCACGAATTTAATTGAAATCCTTCTTTTCTCAC

80% match to silver carp on 154 nucleotide portion of sequence